Is St. Thomas's Aristotelian
Philosophy of Nature Obsolete?

Is St. Thomas's Aristotelian Philosophy of Nature Obsolete?

Robert C. Koons

ST. AUGUSTINE'S PRESS
South Bend, Indiana

Manufactured in the United States of America.

paperback ISBN: 978-1-58731-432-2
ebook ISBN: 978-1-58731-433-9

1 2 3 4 5 6   27 26 25 24 23 22 22

**Library of Congress Control Number:
2022937219**

TABLE OF CONTENTS

Introduction[1]

Quantum mechanics is one of the most successful theories in the history of science. In some form, it is here to stay. The discovery of the quantum in the early twentieth century has transformed our understanding of the natural world in ways that few have fully grasped. In fact, the quantum revolution is a wholesome development from a theological perspective, reconciling our scientific view of the world with the possibility of human agency.

The Greek philosopher Aristotle (382–322 BC) had a theory of nature that offered a number of advantages from the viewpoint of both humanism and biblical theology. While

1   I want to acknowledge gratefully the support of the James Madison Program at Princeton University, who supported my research in 2014–15, enabling me to initiate the research program presented in this book.

Aristotle recognized a profound difference between human beings and other "substances," based on our unique rationality, he avoided Platonic dualism, and he conceived of human aspirations as continuous with the striving of all natural things to their essential ends, providing an objective basis for norms in ethics, aesthetics, and politics.

Aristotelianism has undergone a great revival in the intervening 40 years, with Aristotelian approaches to ethics, both in terms of virtue ethics (e.g., Alasdair MacIntyre and John McDowell) and in the natural goodness theories of Philippa Foot and Michael Thompson, and with stalwart defenses of Aristotle's approach to science by David Charles, James Lennox, Michail Peramatzis, and others. Hylomorphism of a sort has gained wide acceptance in contemporary metaphysics.

Is Aristotelian Natural Philosophy Necessary?

But this revival would seem to be ill-fated unless we can somehow overcome the challenge from modern science. Aristotle's hylomorphism, his theory of form and matter, appears both in his *Physics* and in his *Metaphysics*. It is a theory that bridges the divide between the philosophy of nature and metaphysics proper. So, we must ask two questions: can we have an Aristotelian metaphysics (a theory of being as such) without an Aristotelian philosophy of nature? And can we have an Aristotelian philosophy of nature without Aristotelian natural science? Many Thomists in the twentieth and twenty-first centuries have answered Yes to one or both of these questions, but I believe that the right answer to both is, No.

Those who answer Yes to the first question defend a position we could call *Aristotelianism without hylomorphism*. And those who answer Yes to the second question I call *Aristotelian quietists*. Quietists insist that we must adopt both an Aristotelian metaphysics and an Aristotelian philosophy of nature but insist that this twin adoption has no implications for the practice of the sciences. Consequently, Aristotelian natural philosophy becomes unfalsifiable, justified by common human experience in a way that cannot be unseated by scientific discoveries.

I want to argue for two claims: first, that the theological and philosophical consequences of both anti-hylomorphism and quietism are quite devastating. And, second, that a re-conceiving of contemporary natural science in Aristotelian terms is not only possible but desirable.

Let's consider briefly the consequences of deleting hylomorphism from Aristotelianism, for that matter.

I will mention just two typical examples.

First, transubstantiation. If bread and wine are not hylomorphic, then no instance of bread or wine is *essentially* bread or wine. They are simply congeries of elementary particles, which are at certain times accidentally so arranged as to constitute bread or wine. When Jesus says, "this" is my body, He is therefore referring to the particles, and so it would be the particles that are turned into His Body and Blood. Since these elementary particles never corrupt (at least, not within the time frame of billions or trillions of years), it would follow that transubstantiation is practically irreversible, which would lead to many absurdities in practice.

In addition, elementary particles don't have accidental intrinsic properties, only accidental arrangements in space. Hence, there are no properties that could be sustained in the Host after transubstantiation, and so the appearances of the Host (color, shape, taste, etc.) would have to be mere illusions.

Second, the human soul and body. If nature is not hylomorphic, then the human body consists of a large number of elementary particles arranged *accidentally* in space. The human soul cannot be responsible for the existence or character of these particles, since they are not (in this epoch) capable of generation, corruption, or intrinsic alteration. Consequently, the human soul cannot be the "formal" cause of the body. So, what can the relationship be between soul and body? It must be something like efficient causation only—the soul is merely a motor that moves particles in some extra-physical manner. If so, the body is extrinsic to the soul, and thus the human being consists entirely of the soul alone, with the body as an accidental accoutrement. Abandoning hylomorphism means falling into Cartesian dualism and angelism.

To summarize: if we want a non-dualistic anthropology and a Catholic account of the Eucharist, we need an Aristotelian philosophy of nature.

So, hylomorphism seems to be non-negotiable for Catholics. Can we have a hylomorphic philosophy of nature while accepting an anti-Aristotelian natural science? The quietist strategy typically follows Jacques Maritain in distinguishing natural philosophy from what he called *empiriological* science. On this picture, our natural philosophy must be hylomorphic, but natural science need not be, because the methods or aims of the two are disjoint. Personally, I don't think that the methodological and epistemological distinctions between "ancient" natural philosophy and "modern" natural science are in fact clear or deep.

Aristotelian natural philosophy is and always has been empirical in nature. It's certainly not strictly *a priori* in the Kantian sense. It also seems to me a mistake to think of Aristotelian natural philosophy as entirely deductive in nature. It is scientific *explanations* that are deductive, both for Aristotle and for modern science, explanations that occur within a mature science, a science whose discovery is empirical. It is true that Aristotelians add to the empirical side of the epistemology of the science the indispensable role of *Noûs* or understanding, that faculty by which we recognize that we have arrived at a true account of nature. But, given the under-determination of theory by all possible data, every realist epistemology must have some counterpart to *Noûs*, a faculty that enables us to choose wisely and reliably among multiple, empirically equivalent theories.

Did Aristotelian natural philosophy aim for a kind of *certainty* that natural science eschews? I don't see much of a difference here. Many of Aristotle's proposed principles and definitions are clearly tentative, and many of the conclusions of modern science are certain beyond a reasonable doubt.

There does seem to be *some* difference in aims, however. Aristotelian natural philosophy sought to find the *definitions* of substantial essences and accidental quasi-essences, while the modern natural sciences aim at the discovery of simple, mathematical *laws*. But are these really two different ends, or simply the *same* end conceived in two different ways? There is certainly a deep difference between Aristotelian natural philosophy and natural science as conceived of by logical positivists, neo-Humeans, instrumentalists, and pragmatists, but these are erroneous modern theories about modern natural science, not to be identified with modern science itself. Maritain's suggestion that *empiriological* science was a different genus of inquiry made sense during the heyday of logical positivism, but few philosophers of science today would agree that the aim of natural science is simply to produce useful summaries of empirical observations. According to philosophers of science today, modern science shares Aristotle's ambition of explaining natural phenomena in terms of the real essences of things.

In any case, I want to focus here on the first-order description of nature and put aside methodology and epistemology. What would an Aristotelian natural philosophy look like, if it renounced forever the need to be informed by detailed and progressive empirical inquiry? Charles De Koninck gives us some idea. In his 1934 book, *Le Cosmos*, De Koninck (De Koninck 1934) suggested that there are just four "philosophical" species: man, animal, plant, and the inorganic. This would mean that all inorganic substances would share exactly the same nature (or essence). A nature is, for Aristotle, the principle of change and rest, the ultimate foundation for all explanations of natural phenomena. How could rocks, lakes, clouds, beams of light, scatterings of neutrinos, plasma, black holes all share exactly the same nature? And if, as De Koninck admits, inorganic substance is defined negatively, as the absence of life, how can such a negative definition provide any inorganic things with a real nature at all?

How can such generic forms provide inorganic substances with *per se* unity? How can they distinguish one inorganic substance from another? It seems that they cannot, in which case we would have to conclude either that all of inorganic nature constitutes one gigantic substance, or that every fundamental particle constitutes a separate substance. But this will make the emergence of living things utterly mysterious, requiring them to corrupt the naturally incorruptible in order to secure their own matter.

It seems that by "philosophical species" de Koninck must mean something very different from what Aristotle meant. When we turn to human beings, the result would be that human nature would have to be similarly amorphous and plastic. Sexual reproduction and our sexual identities, for example, would be contingent accidents of human beings, and not essential to us, since they follow neither from our rationality nor from our animality as such. This would render Thomistic deductions of the secondary principles of natural laws, such as those governing sexual conduct in the *Secunda Secundae Partis* or the *Summa Contra Gentiles*, unsound.

Is Aristotelian Natural Philosophy Concordant with Modern Science?

What we must have is an Aristotelian philosophy of nature that is informed by and so accountable to detailed empirical investigation. Our natural philosophy should be continuous with our natural science, albeit at a higher level of generality and a deeper level of philosophical explanation. This does inevitably entail that Aristotelian natural philosophy (and so, ultimately, Aristotelian metaphysics) is in principle falsifiable, or at least subject to disconfirmation, by empirical results. Now, I think this is a plus, rather than a minus, since it provides an antidote to the temptation of apriorism in philosophy. And, as it turns out, natural science has not falsified Aristotelian natural philosophy—in fact, it provides strong empirical support for it, especially after the quantum revolution of the early twentieth century.

It is true, that in the so-called "classical" physics and chemistry of the period from Galileo-to-Rutherford, the appearances *seemed* to be against hylomorphism. If the ambitions of the physicalists and materialists of this period had been realized—if all natural phenomena could have been accounted for in terms of the locomotion of uniform, unqualified matter, then the framework of hylomorphism would have had no purchase.

But we must distinguish between *aspiration* and *achievement*. The physicalists aspired to make substantial form superfluous, but they did not in fact *succeed* in doing so. The introduction of gravity by Newton and of electromagnetic charge by Maxwell completely undermined the Democritean uniformity of matter that Galileo, Descartes, Boyle, and Hobbes had hoped for. The discovery of atomic elements and of elementary particles restored Aristotelian species and their definitions to the center of scientific theory. And natural science never achieved a complete reduction of chemical and biological kinds to facts about the movement and arrangement of physical particles. Chemists and biologists continued to appeal to the enduring natures of compounds and organisms in their scientific explanations of the phenomena.

Thus, the conflict was never between hylomorphism and modern science, but rather between hylomorphism and a certain *philosophy* of science—we might even call it an *ideology* of science (in Marx's sense). This ideological ambition was to make fundamental physics play the role of the queen of sciences. But this ambition was never in fact realized, and it crashed catastrophically into the brick wall of quantum phenomena.

The quantum revolution of the last 100 years has transformed the image of physical and chemical nature in profound ways that are not yet fully understood by philosophers or physical scientists. The new image of nature has in fact revived Aristotelian modes of understanding across a wide swath of scientific disciplines, a transformation that has occurred spontaneously and almost without being noticed. As the neo-Aristotelian framework begins to take shape and to rise to the level of common knowledge, thereby influencing our metaphysical imagination, our understanding of our shared human nature and of our place in the cosmos will improve in ways that are quite concordant with classical Christian humanism.

Overview

In chapter 1, I will lay out the principal elements of Aristotle's image of nature, with its multi-leveled world that included real agency at the biological and personal levels. I will then briefly describe the anti-Aristotelian revolution of the seventeenth century and its metaphysical consequences, including the immediate movement toward some form of mind/matter dualism and the subsequent shrinking of the domain of the soul to a vanishing point. The ultimate result of this revolution is the dominance within philosophy of *micro-physicalism*, the thesis that all of material reality is exhausted by the autonomous natures of fundamental particles (or waves) and their spatial and temporal inter-relations.

Before turning to the details of contemporary quantum science, I will sketch the basic requirements of an Aristotelian pluralism in Chapter 2. Aristotelian philosophy of nature maintains a unique balance between top-down (formal) and bottom-up (material) modes of explanation. This balance requires the use of a repertoire of basic Aristotelian concepts, including proximate and prime matter, substantial form, quantitative accidents, and integral and virtual parts.

In Chapter 2, I introduce a notion of "ontological escalation," which corresponds to a relation of partial independence (with respect to metaphysical grounding) between different levels of scale. Ontological escalation stands in direct contradiction to any form of *microphysicalism*, according to which the only metaphysically fundamental entities, properties, and relations occur entirely at the microscopic scale (the scale of simple, non-composite entities). Then I address a problem for the incorporation of quantum physics within the new Aristotelianism: the identification of the members of the category of *substance* (ousiai). I will outline briefly the role that substance plays in Aristotelian metaphysics. Then, I turn to the question of which entities in modern physics can qualify as Aristotelian substances. In particular, I argue that organisms can do so but that artifacts, groups, elementary particles, and the cosmos as a whole cannot. This raises the problem of where to locate the substances in the inorganic world. I offer in response the theory of thermal substances, which I develop in detail in chapters 3 and 4.

My project encompasses three phases, three goals—of increasingly ambitious character.

1. Phase 1: sketch a hylomorphic, neo-Aristotelian interpretation of modern quantum theory, arguing that it represents a genuine and stable location in logical space. This takes place in Chapters 1, 2, and 7.

2. Phase 2: I argue in Chapter 3 that there is no empirical evidence against the hylomorphic interpretation—that it is at least as well supported by data and scientific practice as is the microphysicalist, modern alternative.

3. Phase 3: in Chapters 4 and 5, I argue that the empirical evidence supports the hylomorphic interpretation over the other alternatives, including old Copenhagen, Bohm, objective-collapse, and Everett interpretations.

In chapters 3 through 5, I point out the ways in which the quantum revolution has reversed the advantages enjoyed by micro-physicalism under the Newton-Maxwell regime. Quantum theory reveals a world in which wholes are typically prior to their parts—that is, a world in which either the causal powers or the spatial locations (or both) of micro-particles depend upon the irreducibly holistic features of the systems to which they belong. This is the well-known fact of the non-separability of quantum properties.

I defend an Aristotelian model that draws on two areas of contemporary science: quantum chemistry and thermodynamics (Chapter 3) and the measurement problem (Chapters 4 and 5). A *hylomorphic* (from Aristotle's concepts of *hyle*, matter, and *morphe*, form) interpretation of quantum thermodynamics and chemistry, in which parts and wholes stand in a mutually determining relationship, better fits both the empirical facts and the actual practice of scientists. I argue that only a hylomorphic interpretation of QM is able to treat thermodynamic quantities, such as temperature and entropy, as genuinely real, which in turn provides grounds for the reality of the direction of time and of molecular structure.

I argue that the distinction between commuting (quantal) and non-commuting (classical) properties in quantum theory (a distinction that appears only when models are taken to the thermodynamic or continuum limit) provides the basis for a new version of the Copenhagen interpretation, an interpretation that is realist, holistic, and hylomorphic in character. This new version allows for the attribution of fundamental causal powers (both active and passive) to meso- and macroscopic entities, including human observers and their instruments.

In Chapter 4, I turn to this *measurement problem* in quantum mechanics, which has created a situation in which it is now quite unclear how the familiar "classical" properties (like spatial position) of the macroscopic objects that we can observe relate to the quantum states of their ultimate constituents. Quantum mechanics is thus open to multiple, empirically equivalent *interpretations*, some of which simply deny that macroscopic objects are wholly derivative, obtaining their macroscopic properties by a mere summation of the properties of their parts.

I turn, in Chapter 5, to one of the most popular interpretations of quantum mechanics in recent years: the Everettian many-worlds interpretation. I examine, more specifically, the most sophisticated version of this interpretation, created by the Oxford

Introduction

school, led by David Wallace. I argue there
that the Oxford Everettians fail to provide an
adequate account of the meaning of quantum
probabilities. In addition, their attempt to pull
off a simultaneous double reduction—of the
macroscopic physical world to the appearance
of "real patterns" in our experience, and of
the mind to the physical—results in a radical
indeterminacy of thought and meaning. Consequently, there remains no metaphysical difference between the manifest image of
everyday life and any logically consistent
story, no matter how fantastic.

I look at the implications of the Aristotelian model of quantum mechanics for our
understanding of biology and of the human
sciences in Chapter 6. This model can provide
an explanation for the existence of irreducibly
biological causal powers and teleology, which
are essential to preserving biology's status as
a genuine science. I argue, relying on joint
work by Alex Pruss and myself, that current
attempts to reduce biology and biological teleology to behavioral functions and evolutionary history fail, and that only an Aristotelian
model is likely to succeed.

Finally, I develop the hylomorphic model in order to deal with some empirical facts about remnants and vestiges of substances in Chapter 7. This requires an examination of both accidents and quantitative parts of substances.

Chapter 1
The Rise and Fall
of Physicalism

1.1 The Aristotelian Tradition

In Aristotle's philosophy of nature, as developed in his *Physics* and *Metaphysics*, all material things have two metaphysical factors or grounds: their *matter* and their *form*. The matter of a thing consists of its parts or components: the matter of a mixture is the elements that compose it, and the matter of an organism is made up of its discrete parts. There is really no such thing as *matter* as such (except as a kind of useful fiction or limiting-case idealization, so-called "prime" matter). Instead, *matter* is a relative term: the many parts and components are (collectively) *the matter of* the whole they compose.

There are, correspondingly, two fundamental kinds of explanation or causation: formal and material. Material explanation is bottom-up: we explain the characteristics of a whole in terms of the way in which the characteristics of its parts and their relations to each other constrain how the whole must be. We can explain the flammability of a book in terms of the flammability of its pages, and we can explain the shape of one of the Great Pyramids in terms of the spatial relations among its constituent blocks of stone.

Formal causation, in contrast, is top-down. To give the formal cause of a thing is to elucidate its essence, the what-it-is-to-be a thing of its kind. The essence of a composite thing constrains and partially determines the natures and mutual relations of its parts. The essence of each part depends (to some degree, at least) on the essence of the whole in which it participates. For example, to be a heart is to be an organ that plays a certain role in an organism's circulatory system. To be *flesh* is to be organic material that participates actively in the organic functions of an animal. To be *a gene* is to be part of a DNA molecule that codes for the production of certain proteins in the natural cellular activity of the cell. And so on.

Once we have the formal and material causes of complete material things (which Aristotle called ousiai or *substances*), we can predict and explain how they will interact. That is, we will have an account of the active and passive causal powers of things: what changes they can cause in others and what changes they can undergo themselves. This way of accounting for change—namely, change as the result of the exercise of causal powers, rooted in the forms or essences of the agent and patient involved—is called *efficient* causation. The Aristotelian model of efficient causation does not simply seek to describe the changes as conforming to some abstract laws of nature or of motion (as is the case in much modern philosophy, following the lead of Hume) but rather attempts to understand the changes as expressions of the formal and material causes of the entities involved in the interaction. In part, this is because Aristotle conceives of time as the product of change, and not vice versa. It is essences (the formal causes) of things that propel time forward by inducing change and initiating activities. Unlike early modern philosophers, Aristotle did not think of change as the by-product of the inexorable forward movement of time and the guidance of abstract and global laws of nature.[2]

The Aristotelian conception of efficient causation through causal powers allows for the existence of exceptional situations: situations in which the causal power of one substance is frustrated or distorted by the action of another substance, or by the absence of one of its natural preconditions. It is natural in an Aristotelian framework to speak of the *malfunctioning* of a substance when its causal powers are blocked or disabled. In addition, a complex substance can become more or less *denatured*, losing (perhaps permanently) some of the causal powers that define its natural

2   See Cartwright (1983) and (1994) for a defense of the Aristotelian model of efficient causation, in light of modern experimental science.

kind. This loss of characteristic powers can be identified with the phenomenon of being *damaged*. We can further distinguish between a substance's normal and abnormal environment by identifying which external conditions do or do not damage or disable it.

Final causation or teleology—the universal directedness of things to their natural "ends"—readily follows from this Aristotelian foundation. The active and passive causal powers of a thing have an inherent and ineliminable reference to an ideal future: how things *would* proceed if those powers *were* able to express themselves fully and without interference. As Thomas Aquinas (Aquinas 1947a) puts it in the *Summa Theologiae* (Part I, Q44, A4): "Every agent acts for an end: otherwise one thing would not follow more than another from the action of the agent, unless it were by chance." This applies even to inanimate agents. David Armstrong referred to this as the "proto-intentionality" of causal powers (Armstrong 1999, 138–40), and George Molnar spoke in such cases of "physical intentionality" (Molnar 2003, 60–66). Thus, the intentionality of human desires and aspirations (their being about some possible, ideal future) is perfectly continuous with the proto-intentionality of all Aristotelian substances, whether animate or inanimate, conscious or non-conscious, rational or sub-rational.

In particular, as Aristotle notes (*Parts of Animals* I, i, 640b-641b, Aristotle 1937), the heterogeneous parts of animals require explanation in terms of their end (telos). Teleology in biology is simply the application to living things of Aristotle's general scheme of explanation. If organisms truly exist as genuine substances (ousiai), then they must have forms that supply them and their parts with genuine, irreducibly biological causal powers. As we have seen, to bear causal powers is ipso facto to be ordered to certain kinds of ideal futures. Thus, there is an unbreakable connection between the substantial reality of organisms and the genuineness of biological teleology.

As Georg Toepfer has put it in a recent essay:

> "...teleology is closely connected to the concept of the organism and therefore has its most fundamental

role in the very definition of biology as a particular science of natural objects…. The identity conditions of biological systems are given by functional analysis, not by chemical or physical descriptions…. This means that, beyond the functional perspective, which consists in specifying the system by fixing the roles of its parts, the organism does not even exist as a definite entity." (Toepfer 2012, at 113, 115, 118)

Consequently, in the Aristotelian image of nature, *substances* (metaphysically fundamental things) exist at many levels of scale and composition. For this reason, we cannot give a complete description of the material world by simply aggregating a large number of microscopic descriptions. Exclusive attention to the microscopic scale will necessarily leave out many crucial facts about the natures of macroscopic substances and the causal powers that derive from these macroscopic natures.

Aristotelians can thus acknowledge real and irreducible agency at many different levels of scale: chemical, thermodynamical, biological, and socio-political, as well as micro-physical. In particular, the rational agency of human beings is not threatened by their complete materiality. The macroscopic behavior of the whole human being is not merely a by-product or *epiphenomenon* of the interactions of his microscopic parts and those of his environment. The human being as such, including a rational sensitivity to the true value of things, makes a real contribution to the flow of events in the material world, without requiring any interaction between the body and some separate, wholly immaterial soul. For Aristotelians, the human soul is the form of the living human body.

1.2 The Anti-Aristotelian Revolution

From the late Middle Ages (after the death of Thomas Aquinas) through the Scientific Revolution and the birth of modern philosophy in the seventeenth century, Western Europeans abandoned three key elements of the Aristotelian system. First, beginning with Duns Scotus, they replaced Aristotle's matter-form relation with the early modern conception of *matter as such*, as something with an inherent nature of its own. Second, they replaced Aristotle's model of interlocking causal powers (active and passive) and time as the measure of change with a model of abstract laws of motion and a fixed and independent temporal dimension. Third, and consequent to the first two, they abandoned Aristotle's formal and final causation, limiting teleology to the relation between conscious agents and their felt desires and impulses.

The introduction of matter as such

As described by Richard Cross (Cross 1998, 74–77), the scholastic philosopher Duns Scotus replaced Aristotle's relational conception of matter (x is the matter of y, or the x's are collectively the matter of y) with a substantive conception of matter, in which matter *as such* has its own determinate nature and causal dispositions. For Aristotle, the relation of matter to form was a relation of potentiality to its actualization: to say that the x's are collectively the matter of y is to say that the x's have the joint potential to compose something of y's nature. Thus, if there were such a thing as pure or prime matter, matter as such, it would be a thing of pure potentiality, with no positive nature of its own.

In contrast, Scotus (and the scholastic philosophers who followed him, including William of Ockham) thought of matter as a kind of thing or stuff, with its own intelligible nature.

Abstract laws of motion

Early modern science and philosophy in the sixteenth century inherited this late-medieval conception of matter as a kind of stuff. The essence of matter was quantitative: all matter takes up a definite volume (by filling a region of space). By taking into account the relative density of matter in its various locations, we can assign to each chunk of matter a certain absolute quantity, which corresponds to something like weight and, eventually, mass.

What about the inherent causal dispositions

of this matter? In this simplest picture (embraced by Descartes), matter has the disposition to move in a constant velocity (by inertia, or conservation of momentum), unless deflected from this movement by a collision with other material bodies. The discovery of gravity and, eventually, of electromagnetic forces spoiled the simplicity of this late-scholastic/early-modern model and in effect re-introduced at the microphysical level instances of something very much like Aristotelian forms (the form of the electron as negatively charged, for example).

This partial recovery of Aristotelian metaphysics was obscured by the simultaneous replacement (in thinkers like Malebranche and Hume) of causal powers by laws of motion. Instead of thinking about bodies as having (by virtue of gravitational mass or electric charge) the *power* of moving and moving other bodies, scientists and philosophers were instead content to describe the regular relationships between inputs and outputs as described by abstract laws of motion, conceived of as "laws of nature."

This shift from hypothesizing natures and their powers to the use of mathematical equations and functions to describe possible motions reflected the earlier pragmatism of Descartes and Francis Bacon. Descartes and Bacon expressed their lack of interest in a deep understanding of why things acted the way they did. They argued that modern science should instead focus simply on predicting and controlling the behavior of things.

> "It is possible to attain knowledge which is very useful in life, and, instead of that speculative philosophy which is taught in the schools, we may find a practical philosophy by means of which, knowing the force and action of fire, water, air, the stars, heavens and all other bodies that environ us... [We can] employ them all in uses to which they are adapted, and thus render ourselves the masters and possessors of nature." (Descartes, *Discourse on Method*, Volume I, 119. See also Bacon 1915, *The Advancement of Learning*, p. 96.)

Rejection of formal and final causation

Once modern philosophers and scientists had replaced talk of causal powers and interactions with abstract laws of motion, quite naturally the concepts of formal and final causation fell into disuse. Laws of motion were supposed to be universal and exceptionless, leaving no room for malfunction or damage.

The pragmatism of philosophers like Descartes and Bacon contributed to the removal of teleology from natural science. Understanding the natural end of something contributed nothing to our control over it. Control required merely a detailed knowledge of the internal disposition of its matter, in such a way that laws of motion could be used to predict and control its behavior. Attention to natures, causal powers, and inherent directedness were merely distractions from this urgently needed project:

> "But this misplacing hath caused a deficience, or at least a great

improficience in the sciences themselves. For the handling of final
causes, mixed with the rest in physical inquiries, hath intercepted the
severe and diligent inquiry of all
real and physical causes, and given
men the occasion to stay upon
these satisfactory and specious
causes, to the great arrest and prej-
udice of farther discovery." (Francis Bacon 1915, *The Advancement
of Learning*, p. 98)

The French biologist Claude Bernard
(1813–1878) clearly expressed the modern
attitude in saying, "The final cause does not
intervene as an actual and efficacious law of
nature." (Bernard 1966, p. 336) Bernard
cannot conceive of any causation except
that expressed by abstract laws. He drew
the logical consequence: "Vital properties
are in reality only the physicochemical
properties of organized matter." (Bernard
1966, pp. 22–23) (Quoted by Gilson and
translated by John Lyon, Gilson 1984, pp.
35–36.)

The dualism of modernity: A fractured world

If the natural world consists entirely of a (more or less) uniform "matter," and if this matter simply obeys universal, exceptionless "laws," what place is left for human thought and human agency? Beginning with scholastic philosophers like Duns Scotus, European thinkers began moving away from the Aristotelian hylomorphism of Thomas Aquinas toward some form of mind-body dualism. Scotus and Ockham, followed by Bacon and Descartes, explicitly limited the scope of teleology and purpose to the conscious desires of human egos, egos that are now radically divorced from the world of matter.

The Soul of the Gaps: The abolition of human agency and teleology

However, this dualism of the late scholastic and early modern world did not constitute a stable position but quickly collapsed into an austere form of materialism. Dualism introduced a kind of "soul of the gaps": mental entities as an extraneous, adventitious addition to the scientific worldview, introduced simply to explain those features of human life and experience that science has not (yet) explained in terms of the motions of matter. As we gained a more and more complete understanding of the operations of the brain, of the nerve cells that make up the brain, and of the organic molecules that make up those cells, there seemed to be less and room for the intervention of immaterial souls of the Cartesian kind. Eventually, a more austere and monistic form of materialism took hold, pioneered by Thomas Hobbes, by French thinkers like d'Holbach, and by the German materialists of the nineteenth century.

This materialism ultimately takes the form of *micro-physicalism*, the thesis that every truth (causal and otherwise) about any macroscopic substance is wholly grounded in and explained by the microphysical facts, including both the intrinsic properties of the micro-particles and binary spatial relations among their positions and velocities in a uniform and rigid background of absolute space. Moreover, this grounding of macroscopic truths in microscopic facts licenses an ontological *reduction* of macroscopic things to their microphysical parts and their spatial relations: the former are *nothing over and above* the latter.

One important aspect of the scientific revolution of the seventeenth and eighteenth centuries was its emphasis on what the Aristotelian would label material causation and explanation through *hypothetical necessity*. If large systems are to behave as they are observed to do, they must be composed of parts with intrinsic natures and mutual arrangements in space that are capable of sustaining the observed collective behavior. From an Aristotelian point of view, this analytic approach is perfectly legitimate. It is illuminating to learn that water is composed of H_2O molecules, and that cells contain double helices of DNA.

Where, from an Aristotelian point of view, micro-physicalism goes wrong is in insisting that macroscopic phenomena can be *exhaustively* explained in terms of microphysical facts. Microphysicalists assume that all facts are wholly determined by the microphysical entities and their arrangements in space. This is true both of atomists of various kinds and those who believe that matter is infinitely divisible, like Empedocles or Descartes. according to this view, the motions of large bodies depend on their composition and on the motions of those components, and not vice versa. All true explanation on this view is bottom-up, from the very small to the large, and never top-down.

This means that for the microphysicalist, there can be no room for substantial form—with one possible exception. If there are fundamental, indivisible particles, they and they alone could have substantial form. Anti-atomists like Descartes or Empedocles must reject substantial forms altogether, since in their view there are no true unities in nature, merely uniform and infinitely divisible continua.

In any case, neither people nor organisms more generally nor any of the many things that we can perceive have substantial forms at all, in this view. Consequently, micro-physicalists must deny the reality of all the so-called secondary qualities, such as color, smell, or taste. Even the primary qualities (as perceived by us) are put in a perilous condition (as Bishop Berkeley first recognized). It's not surprising that some contemporary heirs of microphysicalism deny the reality of space and time themselves.

Long before the quantum revolution, this anti-realism about the "manifest image" of the world (to use Wilfred Sellars's phrase) threatened to undermine the scientific enterprise itself, since all of our observations and experiments presuppose the real existence of, well, observations and experiments, neither of which can easily be accommodated by a microphysicalist image of the world. Experiments require experimental conditions or setups, and these are definable only in macroscopic terms. If the macroscopic world is merely a world of misleading appearances, how are experiments possible?

This micro-physicalism, common to both ancient materialists like Democritus and Lucretius and modern physicalists like Quine or David Lewis, has always stood in some tension with our common-sense understanding of us as *rational agents*. For example, in the *Phaedo*, Plato puts into Socrates' mouth an argument against metaphysical microphysicalism (98c–99b).

"And it seemed to me it was very much as if one should say that Socrates does with intelligence whatever he does, and then, in trying to give the causes of the particular thing I do, should say first that I am now sitting here because my body is composed of bones and sinews, and the bones are hard and have joints which divide them and the sinews can be contracted and relaxed and, with the flesh and the skin which contains them all, are laid about the bones; and so, as the bones are hung loose in their ligaments, the sinews, by relaxing and contracting, make me able to bend my limbs now, and that is the cause of my sitting here with my legs bent... and should fail to mention the *real causes*, which are, that the Athenians decided that it was best to condemn me, and therefore I have decided that it was best for me to sit here and that it is right for me to stay and undergo whatever penalty they order." (Plato 2002)

Microphysicalists have essentially three options in response to this argument: (i) they can deny the existence of real or objective values altogether (the goodness of Socrates' remaining in Athens), (ii) they can assert that our intentions or decisions are never really sensitive to these objective values (Socrates' rational appreciation of this value), or (iii) they can claim that objective values and our sensitivity to them are somehow wholly grounded in the microphysical facts. None of these three seems promising. Jonathan Dancy (2003), Christina Korsgaard (1986), and many others in recent years have created powerful objections to a Humean subjectivism about value. And, in any case, it seems that subjective values must ultimately be grounded in objective value, if reason is to have any normative force at all. Even if one supposes that particular things are good for an agent only because he or she desires them, one must still suppose that desires are the sort of thing that (other things being equal) *ought to be* satisfied—that there is something objectively worthy about seeking to satisfy them.

Finally, as J. L. Mackie and others have recognized (Mackie 1977), it is hard to believe that the objective value or to-be-sought-ness of certain states or actions could be wholly grounded in the sort of facts described by micro-physics. Micro-physics provides no room for the rational teleology of human values.

1.3 The Quantum Revolution

So, there were always grounds for suspicion about the microphysicalist ambition but the success for so long of what is now called "classical physics," the physics of Newton and Maxwell, and even of the theories of relativity, suggested that such a picture *must* be true, whatever its philosophical and epistemological conundrums. This changes dramatically with the quantum revolution. The revolution has not perhaps made microphysicalism *completely* untenable, but it has clearly put it on the defensive and opened up the *live* possibility of resurrecting substantial forms at macroscopic scales, including the scale of human beings and other organisms.

The Revival of Potentiality

It was Werner Heisenberg who first recognized the connection between quantum theory and Aristotle. He wrote, in *Philosophy and Physics* (in 1958), that quantum theorists had simply re-discovered Aristotle's concept of *potentiality*. Heisenberg got it exactly right. Prior to the quantum revolution, scientists treated the domain of potentiality as merely a useful fiction—a realm of mathematically conceivable possibility, the world of the thought experiment. The real world, in contrast, was supposed to consist exclusively of the actual—an infinite sequence of actual positions and momenta, linked together by deterministic natural laws. In sciences that seemed *prima facie* to depend on objective probability or chance, like thermodynamics or natural selection, the appeal to chance was believed to be reducible to epistemology, to our relative ignorance of those exact positions and momenta.

Quantum theory changed all that. In quantum theory, you cannot explain what actually happens without appealing to what was merely potential in nature. For example, in Feynman's sum over histories technique, one's empirical predictions must take into account the sum total of the potential paths of each particle, regardless of which of those paths (if any) were actually taken.

The Return of Teleology

And, once we have potentiality in the frame, we automatically gain teleology. Every potentiality, as we know, is intrinsically ordered to some determinate end. And we find a counterpart to this in quantum theory, in the form of least-action principles, and, in quantum thermodynamics and chemistry, in the form of increasing entropy and the movement toward equilibrium. As I will argue below, quantum thermodynamics gives us a universal, objective, and intrinsic direction to time. The combination of real potentialities with a real direction of time yields real teleology.

Classical mechanics can be formulated in either of two ways: in terms of differential equations based on Newton's laws of motion, or in terms of integral equations in terms of the conservation of energy (the analytic or

Lagrangian method). In the latter case, the structure of the model imposes certain constraints on the possible evolution of the system, and the dynamical laws pick out the actual evolution on the basis of some minimization (or maximization) principle, like the principle of *least action*. (See Yourgrau and Mandelstam 1968, pp. 19–23, 164–67; Lindsay and Morgenaw 1957, pp. 133–36; Lanczos 1986, pp. xxvii, 345–46.)

The Newtonian model is Democritean, but the Lagrangian is Aristotelian, in being both essentially holistic and teleological. The total energy of a closed system is an irreducibly holistic or non-separable property of the system: it cannot be reduced to the intrinsic properties of the system's constituents, taken individually. More importantly, variational principles like the least action principle treat the holistic character of an entire trajectory as fundamental, rather than the set of instantaneous facts about the composition of forces that constitutes the fundamental facts for the Newtonian model. The least-action principle is a form of teleological explanation, as Leibniz already recognized (McDonough 2008, 2009).

In classical mechanics, either model can be used, and they are provably equivalent. Hence, classical mechanics leaves the metaphysical question of micro-physicalism vs. hylomorphism unresolved. However, with the quantum revolution, the Lagrangian picture becomes mandatory, since the fundamental entities can no longer be imagined to be moving in response to the composition of forces exerted at each moment from determinate distances. Teleology reigns supreme over mechanical forces, as Max Planck noted. (See Planck 1936, pp. 119–26; Planck 1960; Dusek 2001; Thalos 2013, pp. 84–86.) In addition, *the total energy and action of a closed system are essentially holistic or non-separable properties of that composite system*, which stands in contradiction to the demands of micro-physicalism.

In addition, by forcing reliance on the Lagrangian model, quantum mechanics brings into sharper relief the holistic character of causal interaction. As noted by Tiehen and Kronz (2002), the Hamiltonian for complex quantum systems is non-separable: "In that case, the time evolution of the density operator that is associated with a part of a composite system cannot in general be characterized in a way that is independent of the tie evolution of the whole." (Kronz and Tiehen 2002, pp. 343–44) The causal power responsible for the evolution of the system is an irreducibly joint power, not supervening on the binary causal powers of the component particles.

Aristotelian philosophy of nature requires processes as the natural results of the exercise of causal powers. These Aristotelian processes (kinhses) have intrinsic direction and pacing.[3] Aristotle did not, as his late medieval and

3 Schulman (1989) draws out a fascinating parallel between Aristotle's account of motion as "potential" and "indeterminate" in *Physics* III and *Metaphysics* III and Richard Feynman's sum-over-possible-histories approach to quantum mechanics. Aristotle denies that the location of a moving body is fully *actual* except at the beginning and end of a continuous process of locomotion. Feynman's sum-over-histories approach is a way of fleshing this out: the moving body takes every possible trajectory between the two points, with mutual interference explaining why the paths with least action predominate.

early modern critics supposed, anthropomorphize nature by attributing vague "urges" or "drives"; rather, he developed a framework within which animal and human drives could be seen as special cases of the intrinsic directedness of holistic processes. The system as a whole consequently acquires its own intrinsic teleology (or, better, *entelechy*).

Non-Separable States

The most obvious blow that quantum mechanics strikes to micro-physicalism comes from the undeniable *non-separability* of the quantum properties of entangled systems. As noted by Teller (1986), Healey (1991), Silberstein and McGeever (1999, pp. 186–90), Kronz and Tiehen (2002, pp. 325–30), along with many others, the quantum state of a pair of entangled particles (particles in the singlet state, as in the Einstein-Podolsky-Rosen thought experiment) is irreducibly a state of the pair as such: it is not even determined by the intrinsic properties of the particles (considered individually) or the spatial distance or relative velocity between them. In these cases, the whole is literally more than the sum of its parts.

For a long time, philosophers assumed that this sort of quantum weirdness could be limited somehow to the microscopic domain, being almost completely swamped at the phenomenological level by phenomena that completely conform to the requirements of microphysicalism. However, it turns out that this kind of quantum holism is very much the rule rather than the exception, producing measurable results at the phenomenological level nearly all the time (Primas 1980, p. 41).

The Measurement Problem

The so-called "Copenhagen" interpretation (the interpretation given quantum theory by Bohr and other pioneers) gives us reason to doubt all three of these premises. In the Copenhagen interpretation, the microphysical facts consist merely in the attribution to microscopic entities of certain potentialities, and these potentialities essentially include causal relations to macroscopic systems. A quantum doesn't typically have any position or momentum at all (not even a vague or fuzzy one): it has merely the potential to interact with macroscopic systems as if it had some definite position or momentum (or other observable feature) at the moment of the interaction. Thus, the quantum world (so understood) can be neither metaphysically fundamental nor a complete basis for the macroscopic world.

Of course, this situation gives rise immediately to a puzzle: what, then, is the relationship between the macroscopic and quantum worlds? Presumably, macroscopic physical objects are wholly composed of quanta. How, then, can the quanta fail to be metaphysically fundamental and complete basis for the macroscopic world?

Hylomorphism offers a ready answer to this puzzle. The microscopic constituents of macroscopic objects have (at the level of actuality) only an indirect relation to space and time: they are located (roughly) somewhere at a time only *qua* constituents of some fundamental, macro- or mesoscopic substance (in the Aristotelian sense). Such microscopic objects are not metaphysically fundamental in their entirety, and their metaphysically fundamental features do not provide a complete basis for the features of the substantial wholes they compose. This is a welcome result, since it makes physical theory compatible with the *Phaedo* argument.

The Copenhagen interpretation is not the only way to make sense of quantum mechanics. Recent years have seen the emergence of the many-worlds (Everett) interpretation, Bohm's mechanics, and various objective collapse theories. The very fact that we face now a plethora of competing interpretations of quantum mechanics puts the relationship between physics and metaphysics on a very different footing from the one they had under the classical paradigm. Micro-physicalism was the only plausible interpretation of classical physics. In contrast, some interpretations of quantum mechanics are extremely friendly to hylomorphism. I will sketch one of these, which I will call "Pluralistic Quantum Hylomorphism."

Pluralistic Quantum Hylomorphism is an interpretation inspired by some remarks of Heisenberg (1958), and defended by Wolfgang Smith (2005), Nancy Cartwright (1999) and Stanley Grove (2008). In this view, the world consists of a variety of domains, each at a different level of scale. Most of these domains are fully classical, consisting of entities with mutually compatible or commutative properties. At most one domain is accurately described by quantum mechanics. Since location does not (for quantum objects) "commute" with other observables, like momentum, the quantum objects are only intermittently located in ordinary, three-dimensional space, although they always retain a probability of interacting with classical objects at a definite location. Interaction between quantum properties and classical properties (including those of experimenters and their instruments) precipitates an objective collapse of the quantum object's wavefunction, as a result of the joint exercise of the relevant causal powers of the object and the instruments, and not because of the involvement of human consciousness and choice.

Paul Feyerabend offered a helpful tripartite distinction of philosophies of science: the positivist, the realist, and the structural (Feyerabend 1983). The positivist is the anti-realist, who denies that reality has any structure that is independent of our interests and assumptions, the "realist" believes that there is a single, unified structure of reality, realized at a single scale, and the structuralist takes reality to comprise a plurality of relatively autonomous structures. The realist or monist perspective contributed to the rise and development of modern science, but the quantum revolution has seen a return to the pluralism of Aristotle:

> "Einstein and especially Bohr introduced the idea that [scientific] theories may be context-dependent, different theories being valid in different domains. Combining these ideas with abstract mathematics such as various algebras, lattice theory, and logics then led to a powerful revival of the structural approach. Thus the search for a generalized quantum theory is exactly in Aristotle's spirit: we do not take it for granted that the quantum theories we have are the best way of dealing with everything, looking either for new interpretations or suitable approximation methods to solve hairy cases; we

rather try to identify domains and theories suited for them and then look for ways of relating these theories to each other." (Feyerabend 1983, vii)

Here is how Nancy Cartwright describes this pluralist view:

"...quantum realists should take the quantum state seriously as a genuine feature of reality and not take it as an instrumentalist would, as a convenient way of summarising information about other kinds of properties. Nor should they insist that other descriptions cannot be assigned besides quantum descriptions. For that is to suppose not only that the theory is true but that it provides a complete description of everything of interest in reality." (Cartwright 1999, p. 232)

Thus, the hylomorphic interpretation combines features of both the old Copenhagen and newer objective collapse interpretations.

It is a fully realist view about the microscopic, unlike Bohr's version of the Copenhagen interpretation, and it is ontologically pluralistic, in contrast to other objective collapse theories. It admits a plurality of objective domains, and it doesn't treat wave collapse as a phenomenon explainable within the pure quantum domain, by some as-yet-unknown microphysical interaction.

Unlike the Copenhagen view, the PQHM interpretation fully embraces the reality of quantum objects and quantum states. In addition, the Copenhagen view suffers from being too narrowly dualistic, distinguishing the classical world from the quantum world. In contrast, the hylomorphic interpretation embraces a salutary kind of ontological pluralism, recognizing that the non-quantum or supra-quantum world is itself a "dappled" world (as Nancy Cartwright puts it), dividing naturally into multiple domains at multiple scales.

Pluralistic Quantum Hylomorphism shares two crucial advantages with the Copenhagen view. First, it embraces realism about classical objects and classical states, and so it can make sense of our experimental practices in a straightforward way. Second, it fits the actual practice of scientists well, who are in practice ontological pluralists (as Nancy Cartwright has documented).

1.4 Prima Facie Tensions between Aristotle and Quantum Theory

There are several points at which quantum theory may seem to be in conflict with tenets of Aristotelian philosophy. However, each of these tensions can be resolved with only secondary or tertiary changes in the Aristotelian model of nature.

Violations of the Law of Non-Contradiction or Excluded Middle

In the classic two-slit experiment, individual electrons seem to take multiple, incompatible paths between the source and the screen, going simultaneously through both the right and left slit of the barrier. It is only when the electron is detected at the screen that the wave-function "collapses" into one definite path. The theorem of John S. Bell demonstrated that, if quantum theory is correct, we cannot suppose that individual particles take definite paths—that is, we cannot assume that quantum probabilities merely reflect our ignorance of which path is actual. Some take quantum theory to require a revision of classical logic: either supposing that the electron *both is and is not* passing through the left slit (violating the law of non-contradiction), or that the electron *neither is nor is not* passing through that slit (violating the law of excluded middle).

However, from the perennial philosophy, these erroneous conclusions result from failing to distinguish between actuality and *potentiality* (or act and potency, to use the traditional terms). The electron is not a substance—it is rather a feature or an *action* of the substantial source that generates the electrons. This action has the unactualized potential of affecting both the left and right slit simultaneously. However, when actualized, the electron will always be in exactly one place at each time.

Werner Heisenberg first noted (Heisenberg 1958) that quantum mechanics had simply revived Aristotle's notion of potentiality. In pre-quantum physics, we did not need to refer to potentialities at all. We could simply describe and predict the actual trajectories of particles using deterministic laws of motion. In quantum theory, as in Aristotle's philosophy of nature, a complete description of nature requires us to include also the merely potential states and locations of things.

Violations of the Causal Principle: Natural Ex Nihilo?

All quantum theory incorporates a dimension of indeterminism. We can never predict with certainty where and when a quantum effect will be detected by our instruments, even if we were to know all of the physical facts with perfect precision, and even if we were able to perform all necessary calculations instantaneously. The world's evolution is irreducibly *probable* in nature.

But being undetermined should not be confused with being *uncaused*, as Elizabeth

Anscombe pointed out in her inaugural Cambridge lecture (Anscombe 1981). Aristotle's philosophy of nature always recognized that rational agents could act indeterministically. Quantum mechanics has simply revealed that natural agents are more like rational agents than Aristotle had supposed.

Here is an extreme case of this indeterminism: the spontaneous appearance of virtual particles in the quantum vacuum. At first glance, this seems a violation of the ancient principle Ex Nihilo Nihil Fit (nothing comes from nothing). However, appearances are deceiving.

As I will argue in Chapter 2, quantum particles, including virtual particles, are not substances. They are only *potential actions* of substances. When a virtual particle is produced in the so-called vacuum, the particle is generated by a quantum field, which represents the potential action of one or more thermal substances in the environment. When a virtual particle is detected, the detector helps to actualize some active power of these substances. The causal principle is fully respected at all times.

Non-Local Spookiness

As John Bell's theorem demonstrated, quantum mechanics requires a certain kind of instantaneous influence at unlimited distances. This is illustrated by the Einstein-Podolsky-Rosen (EPR) thought experiment, in which a decision about what property to measure at one point in space can have an instantaneous effect on the probabilities of various results at a distant measurement site. This is a serious problem for mechanistic forms of materialism, which is why it worried Einstein so much, but it poses no difficulty at all for Aristotelians. Aristotle believed in instantaneous influence at a distance: he thought, for example, that a light source illuminates an extended body of air instantaneously. Aristotle was wrong about the propagation of light, but he was right in thinking that one substance can have acted instantaneously on a distant substance. The power of a substance to act propagates outward at a velocity no greater than the speed of light, but the actualization of a power at one point in space can affect instantaneously the way in which that same power manifests itself at a distant point.

Chapter 2

Hylomorphism and the Quantum World

2.1 Four Metaphysical Options and Two Philosophies of Nature

There is a natural class of phenomena that at least appears to involve a sort of physical or natural modality. This class includes three sub-classes: subjunctive and counterfactual conditionals, dispositions and causal powers, and causal laws of nature (see Koons and Pickavance 2017). It would be quite surprising if all three sub-classes included metaphysically fundamental facts, since it seems that some can be defined by or grounded in the others. Consequently, there are four ontological options:

1. Powerism. Causal powers and dispositions are fundamental.
2. Hypotheticalism. Facts expressed by means of subjunctive conditionals are fundamental.
3. Nomism. Causal laws of nature are fundamental.
4. Neo-Humeanism. None of these are fundamental, but all are grounded in the *Humean mosaic* of categorical qualities distributed across spacetime.

Hypotheticalism and Nomism have largely fallen out of favor. Hypotheticalism has waned because of the implausibility of the idea that anything fundamentally real corresponds to the world-selection function needed for the semantics of the subjunctive conditional. The relative *closeness* of two worlds seems too subjective and anthropocentric to be a metaphysical primitive. Nomism has faded because of the difficulty of bridging the gap between facts about laws and facts about particular patterns of fact. Bridging this gap means attributing an odd sort of *causal power* to the laws themselves. Thus, the two main competitors today are Powerism (or the *powers ontology*) and Neo-Humeanism.

Neo-Humeanism has gradually declined somewhat in popularity as it failed to provide adequate accounts of the directionality of time and causality, of dispositions and powers, of objective probability, and of scientific theory choice and induction (again, see Koons and Pickavance 2017). Hence, there has been increasing interest in a Powerist alternative. (Of course, I am not denying that the other three views have their contemporary defenders, nor am I claiming that the issue is a settled one.)

A viable powers ontology must include two additional elements: forms and processes. It is processes that *manifest* powers, and it is forms that *ground* them. Causal powers come in two kinds: active and passive. An active power initiates a process of change (kinesis) in some entity, and a passive power is the potentiality for undergoing such a process.

Powers appear in nature in natural clusters, and these power-clusters are the expression of the presence of Aristotelian *forms* (Inman 2018). Functionally equivalent or interchangeable forms constitute the basis of natural kinds of substances, whether essential or accidental. Without forms as the common ground of these repeatable clusters of powers, we would be left with a large number of massive brute coincidences. The substantial form of water explains why the active and passive powers associated with all instances of water are found so regularly in concert.

Active causal powers initiate ongoing processes of change. Without such processes, it would be impossible to explain how the past influences the future, unless we were to posit immediate action at a temporal distance. Processes of change in turn presuppose the existence of fundamentally enduring entities, the fundamental *participants* in these processes, and these participants must be subject to substantial forms that determine their persistence-conditions and their liabilities to accidental change or motion. Nature's repertoire of forms determines what kinds of entities are metaphysically fundamental.

In contrast, the Neo-Humean ontology requires no fundamental processes or fundamentally enduring entities (with their substantial forms). Instead, what is fundamental is a framework of spacetime (or spatiotemporal relations), with regions occupied by one or more kinds of qualities or stuffs (the Humean mosaic). Time is metaphysically prior to change, since change is simply a matter of the appearance of different qualities at different times (Russell's At-At theory of change). Laws of nature are grounded in brute-fact patterns of qualitative succession. On the Mill-Ramsey-Lewis model, a mathematical function counts as a law of nature just in case it is a theorem of the simplest axiomatization of the mosaic's patterns.

The two ontologies of causation correspond closely to two philosophies of nature, philosophies that have been in competition since the later Middle Ages. We can call these the *perennial* (or *scholastic*) and the *modern* philosophies. On the perennial philosophy of nature, the task of science is to identify the substantial and accidental forms in nature, from which flow things' active and passive capacities, which manifest themselves (in turn) in the form of activities and processes of change. Mathematics can be a useful tool in describing these capacities and processes, but science is primarily concerned with discovering the *real definitions* of natural kinds. In addition, the realm of *potentiality* is real and inescapable, even if in some sense dependent on the actual. The reality of potentiality (powers) corresponds to the reality of a kind of teleology: the *natural intentionality* (in George Molnar's phrase) of the real but unmanifested potentialities of nature.

The perennial philosophy of nature is pluralistic, in that each kind of form could give rise to a distinct set of active and passive powers. This allowed for the possibility of fundamental entities studied in distinct theoretical domains, including chemistry and biology as well as physics. In fact, I will go even further and argue that the quantum revolution requires us to *demote* the status of microphysical entities, including particles and fields. We should reverse the usual understanding of *emergence*: it is microphysical phenomena

that emerge from the more fundamental domain of chemistry, thermodynamics, and
solid-state physics, not vice versa.

In the modern view, science is primarily
about discovering fundamental mathematical
relations which *explain* and in some sense
govern observable phenomena. The task is to
find increasingly general and simple formulas,
from which all such mathematical relations
can be derived through calculation. The realm
of potentiality is unreal or imaginary—merely
a result of human thought experiments. Natural reality is exhausted by what actually happens. The modern philosophy of science
aspires to be absolutely unitary, discovering a
single set of laws that apply to all interactions
at all scales. In practice, this translates into the
priority of the microscopic realm, since large-
scale structures and patterns are nothing more
than the sum of their small-scale components.

Aristotle's metaphysics clearly assigns the
status of fundamental to living organisms, despite their intermediate size. Organisms are
neither mere heaps of atoms nor mere frag-
ments of the whole cosmos. They are instead
among the *primary beings* of the world—the

things that have unity and exist in the strictest, most central sense.

Since the Scientific Revolution of the seventeenth century, a kind of philosophical atomism has tended to dominate our understanding of nature. In this view, the power and nature of any composite material entity depends on the powers, natures, and mutual arrangements and motions of the smallest bits of matter. The agency of the particles leaves nothing for reason or free will to do, except in a subordinate and derived way. The atomistic materialist cannot find a place in the world for genuine rational powers, a kind of fundamental responsiveness of the human mind to reasons and evidence.[4]

In response, many theists have embraced a kind interactionist dualism or some form of idealism or cosmic holism (e.g., Rowan Williams—see Pickstock 2015), trying to carve out real space for the domain of reason. However, there are severe theological and

4   See, for example, C. S. Lewis 1947 (chapter 2), Plantinga 2011 (chapter 10), Koons 2017, Koons 2018c, Koons 2019b, and Steward 2012.

apologetic costs to these dualist and idealist stratagems. Both dualists and idealists must posit a problematic explanatory gap between natural phenomena and our internal sensations or "phenomenal qualia" (Levine 2000). The prospects for any simple, law-like relationship between micro-physical properties and sensory qualia are extremely dim, as noted by Robert Adams (1987). Instead, we are left with massively gerrymandered and anomalous correlations between physical conditions and experiential qualities, correlations that can never be illuminated by causal mechanisms. Dualists and idealists also face difficult questions about how spiritual realities can interact with physical processes without violating physical symmetries and conservation laws. Dualists and idealists seem to be stuck with a fruitless quest for some elusive vital force (*élan vital*) by which the mind can move fundamental particles (see Lowe 1992). Ethically, dualists and idealists run the risk of downplaying the importance of bodily integrity, since they make the human body wholly extrinsic to the human person as such (see for example, Lee and George 2009).

If we set aside dualism and idealism as problematic and implausible, then we are forced to choose between the three remaining options: atomism, monism, and pluralism. Atomists hold that only extremely small entities, like subatomic particles or point-intensities of fields, can be metaphysically fundamental, while monists (like Jonathan Schaffer) take that there is only one fundamental entity, the entire cosmos (Schaffer 2010). Pluralists assume that we can find fundamental entities at many different scales of size, including intermediate-sized entities like living organisms. From a classical point of view, there are at least two reasons for favoring pluralism: preserving human agency and securing our knowledge of necessary and normative truths.

First, both physical monism and atomism threaten human agency. If reason is to have any power, the human being must be capable (*sans* reason) to arrive at more than one conclusion (whether theoretical or practical). And which alternative conclusion we do reach must be explainable in terms of our reasons and acts of will—it cannot be exhaustively explained at either the atomic or the cosmic level without introducing an implausible coincidence of over-determination, i.e., an ad hoc, pre-established harmony between the material and the rational (of the sort proposed by Gottfried Leibniz).

Second, for the same reason, monism and atomism threaten human epistemology. Our non-empirical knowledge of necessary facts requires that those facts have some direct impact on our faculty of intuition. The intuitions we form must not be explainable in terms of processes at the atomic or cosmic level, processes with no real, constitutive connection to the relevant necessary facts. This is especially problematic for our knowledge of purely normative facts, since normative facts seem to play no role in determining the nature or movements of either material atoms or the physical cosmos as a whole. Any morality with an intellectual component (anything, that is, beyond the most voluntarist of divine command or social-convention theories) requires both real human agency and real knowledge of normative reasons (see Koons 2019b).

2.2 Hylomorphic Escalation vs. "Emergence"

Hylomorphism and Ontological Escalation.

The term 'emergence' has, I believe, outlived its usefulness, especially since it is now used in such a wide variety of mutually contradictory senses. Consequently, I will define a notion of *ontological escalation*, which is thoroughly metaphysical in nature, as opposed to being epistemological, pragmatic, conceptual, semantic, or logical. Escalation is realized by discrete sets of objects and their properties and relations, not by our theories or understandings of those objects. In defining escalation, I will make free use of the notion of *metaphysical ground*, as discussed recently by Kit Fine and others (Fine 1999, 2012; Rosen 2010), but which is rooted deeply in the philosophical tradition (as far back as Socrates, at the very least).

Thesis of Ontological Escalation

1. The world consists of a number of levels of compositional scale.

2. Except for the very smallest scale, the entities of each scale-level are composed entirely of smaller-scale entities, and the powers of and causally relevant relations among those entities are *partly grounded in* facts about the smaller-scale entities. That is, the larger-scale entities have the causal powers they do in part *by virtue of* their smaller-scale parts and their properties. This corresponds to the hypothetical necessities of material causation.

3. Except for the very largest scale, the powers of and causally relevant relations among *some* entities of each scale-level are *partly grounded in* facts about certain larger-scale entities (namely, those larger-scale entities, the *substances*, of which they are proper, integral parts). This corresponds to formal causation.

Thus, larger-scale entities *both condition and are conditioned by* smaller-scale entities, in relations of mutual metaphysical co-determination.

I will defend in particular a neo-Aristotelian or hylomorphic conception of ontological escalation, in which top-down determination corresponds to Aristotle's notion of formal causation, and bottom-determination corresponds to material causation, building on my paper, "Staunch vs. Fainthearted Hylomorphism" (Koons 2014).

My picture is closest to the models of emergence by fusion proposed by Paul Humphreys (1997). In Humphreys's model, the entities of the smaller-scale levels are literally destroyed in a diachronic process of fusion (the generation of the new, larger-scale entity). This kind of destructive fusion could count as an extreme case of ontological escalation, so long as we consider the "annihilated" *summands* as enjoying some kind of *virtual* or *dependent* existence within the fused entity.

Ontological escalation differs from the model of ontological *emergence* proposed by Timothy O'Connor and his collaborators (O'Connor 1994, O'Connor and Wong 2005), who, like Humphreys, postulate a diachronic process of generation of the emergent entities. In O'Connor-style emergence, the constituents *do* survive the fusion. However, O'Connor supposes that there is some

kind of downward causation involving new
configurational forces (as in C. D. Broad's account—Broad 1925). This comes close to a
kind of vitalism or dualism, and its plausibil-
ity is weakened by our natural reluctance to
posit new fundamental forces. In addition,
O'Connor assumes a kind of original or primordial *universality* of the micro-level, which
must contain in a virtual way all the higher
levels. With ontological escalation, in contrast, all of the levels are equally universal and
primordial (at least potentially). Rather than
imagining that the world began (after the Big
Bang) as a cloud of autonomous particles,
from which larger structures eventually
emerged, I suppose that the early universe
consisted entirely of large-scale substances
(initially, perhaps, a single, cosmic substance),
from which smaller entities gradually precipitated.

2.3 What is it to be a Substance?

Substances are entities that *exist* in the most
central, focal meaning of that analogous
term. To use the language of grounding, the

existence and nature of every other entity are grounded in the existence, nature, and activity of the world's substances. Substances constitute the uniquely fundamental level of reality. As a consequence of this metaphysical fundamentality, substances have *per se* unity to the maximal degree: their unity, both spatially (synchronically) and temporally (diachronically), is metaphysically ungrounded, not dependent on anything else.

Therefore, to the extent that a substance is spatially or materially composite, it must be metaphysically *prior* to its own material parts. Its material (spatially defined) parts are dependent, for their existence, their mutual relations, their intrinsic natures, and their causal agency, on the substantial whole to which they belong.

The nature of substances is also the ultimate ground for temporal change. These natures ground the basic causal powers and potentialities of substances. Substances are among the ultimate source of change in other substances, through the exercise of active causal powers, and the substances contain, in the form of a set of passive powers or potentialities, principles for explaining their own constancy and intrinsic change. In other words, substances contain their own principles of "rest and motion," as Aristotle puts it. The causal laws of nature are, in this view, nothing more than convenient summaries of the sort of changes that substantial natures induce and undergo in various contexts, by virtue of the substances belonging to a relatively sparse set of natural kinds or species. The members of a single species are substances whose natures are functionally equivalent.

This metaphysical model generates what Jonathan Schaffer (2010, 38) has called "the tiling constraint." The tiling constraint consists of two requirements: (i) no two substances overlap, and (ii) everything is wholly contained in the sum of all the substances—that is, every part of every material entity overlaps some substance. The substances of the world are like the tiles that cover a tessellated floor—there are no gaps between substances, and the substances jointly exhaust natural reality.[5]

Many substances (like organisms) interact with their environment *through their parts*. Hence, the powers of the whole substance must in some way be dependent on the disposition of those parts. In addition, the very survival of a substance depends on the appropriate cooperation of its parts. At the same time, there must be something that *unifies* those parts (and just those parts) into a single substance. For Aristotelians, this something is known as a *substantial form*. Each substance has a single substantial form that makes it what it is and that unifies its parts, both at a time and through time.[6] The

---

5   I will argue in Chapter 7 that we must add remnants of substances to the story in order to satisfy the Tiling Constraint.

6   I side here with Thomas Aquinas (and, I believe, with Aristotle himself) in affirming the "unicity" of substantial form: that is, the thesis that every substance has a single substantial form. Some contemporary theorists (e.g., Jaworksi 2016) side instead with Scotus and most later scholastic philosophers in allowing for multiple substantial

substantial form of a substance does **not** simply consist in the nature of its parts and their mutual arrangement in space—it is that which ultimately *grounds and explains* those natures and that arrangement.

For composite, material substances, substantial form cannot be the whole story. There must also be that on which the substantial form operates. This is the substance's *matter*. The primary metaphysical role of matter is that of *individuation*. Chunks of matter individuate a substance and its parts from substances and parts of the same natural kind. They ground the mutual distinctness of things that are specifically the same (the same in kind). This individuating role is what gives the Aristotelian a unique and attractive account of natural sameness (see Brower 2017, Koons 2018d). If we consider matter in its pure function as a bare

forms. They face what I take to be a decisive objection: if the substantial form is that by which everything in the substance (both material parts and accidents) receive their actual existence, then multiple substantial forms would introduce an unacceptable form or over-determination or redundancy in nature.

individuator, we arrive at the concept of *prime matter*. A chunk of prime matter has no positive nature, quality, or quantity of its own. It simply individuates its substance or part of a substance from others of the same kind.[7]

However, prime matter is never wholly on its own, and so never actually bare. It is always of necessity informed by a substantial form, and this informing results in various layers of what is called *proximate matter*.

---

7   My views about the role of matter have changed significantly from my 2014 paper (Koons 2014). I now think that matter's role as an enduring substrate through change (emphasized in Aristotle's *Physics*) is secondary to its more central role as individuator. I now think of the persistence of matter through substantial change as non-fundamental, as the persistence of a kind of *ens successivum* (a series of fundamentally distinct, time-bound entities that are tied together into a kind of causal sequence). Thus, I have moved somewhat in the direction of Scaltsas (1994) and Marmodoro (2013). However, unlike Scaltsas and Marmodoro, I still believe that there are real and not merely conceptual distinctions among a substance, its form, and its matter. The three must be really distinct in order to play three distinct explanatory roles in metaphysics.

The human being, for example, is obviously composed of various kinds of tissue, such as bone, muscle, skin, and blood. Each chunk of tissue corresponds to a chunk of prime matter, but a chunk that has been natured and qualified by the human being's one substantial form. Each piece of proximate matter is composed of parts of more elementary, less proximate kinds of matter. Such intermediate forms of matter in a living organism include proteins, lipids, and carbohydrates, which in turn are composed of still less proximate matter, like carbon, hydrogen, and oxygen, with the most elemental forms of matter (protons, neutrons, electrons) constituting a layer just "above" that of prime matter. It is the one substantial form of the human being (the human soul) that is responsible for the character of each of these layers of matter above the level of prime matter, but each level has an important role to play in explaining the persistence and varying powers of the whole substance. The explanatory role that these layers play is called *material causation*. The substantial form plays the complementary role of *formal causation*.

Given the Tiling Constraint, all parts of substances must be either integral parts or virtual parts. An *integral part* of a substance is a part whose whole nature and individual identity is tied to that substance. My hand, for example, is essentially a hand so essentially a part of a human being. Integral substances can sometimes exist independently of their "host" substance, but they persist only as remnants of that substance and never as substances in their own right. Their natures are such that it is metaphysically impossible for an integral part to exist except as a part or a remnant of a particular substance. Their individual identities are irrevocably tied to the organism from which they originated.

In contrast, *virtual parts* of a substance have intrinsic natures that are independent of the whole. This does not violate the unicity of substantial form, since the virtual parts have *only potential* existence within the whole substance. Moreover, the fact that this inorganic substance can exist as a virtual part of the organism is grounded in the organism's own substantial form.

For any virtual part of a substance, there

are many empirically indistinguishable coun-
terparts existing as actual substances in their
own right and not as mere virtual parts. The
water in my veins, for example, corresponds
chemically and thermodynamically to batches
of water existing in the inorganic world as actual, independent substances. In this case the
Tiling Constraint is satisfied by stipulating
that the virtual part no longer has actual existence while part of my body. It exists only
potentially, contributing to the persistence
and powers of my body but not constituting
at the same time a distinct substance. For this
reason, none of the water in my veins can be
numerically identical to any inorganic sample
of water that I ingested, since the inorganic
water was a substance in its own right and not
merely a virtual part of another substance.
This transmutation of inorganic substances
into virtual parts and vice versa is an unavoid-
able theoretical cost of the hylomorphic picture, but it is a cost well worth paying.

The structured parts of a substance (e.g.,
organs and tissues of the living body) are its
integral parts, while the kinds of stuffs contained by the substance (water, lipids,

proteins, nucleic acids) are or correspond to virtual parts.

Aristotelian natural philosophy includes the reification of certain features of substances—the *accidents*. These accidents are what Keith Campbell called *abstract particulars* (Campbell 1990), corresponding to the *modes* or *tropes* of modern metaphysics. Each accident is simultaneously both a real entity, tied essentially to a single subject, and a feature of that subject. So, Socrates' musicality is a classic example of such an accident. It is *that by which* Socrates is musical. The accident is ontologically dependent on Socrates, and it exactly resembles other instances of the same kind, such as Plato's musicality. These individual accidents can themselves be generated and corrupted, and they enter into other causal and explanatory relations.

The very fact that substances have parts or accidents of any kind is the responsibility of the substantial form. The substantial form is responsible both for providing its integral parts with their natures and with transmuting external inorganic substances into its virtual parts. Substantial form also imposes forms of *quantity* on batches of prime matter—so-called *quantitative accidents* of volume, mass, and relative position. These quantitative accidents stand in part-whole relations to one another. E.g., the location of my left elbow is contained within the location of my left arm. These quantitative accidents are responsible for the possibility of my body's having quantitative or material parts, both integral and virtual. The identities of these quantitative accidents have a dual anchor: tied, in the first place, to the particular substances to which they belong, in the second place, to the particular packet of prime matter that they inform. It is because the quantitative accidents are tied inextricably to the individual identity of the substance to which they belong that all integral parts of the substance are similarly so tied.

2.4 What are the World's Substances?

If we accept the Tiling Constraint, then we must be able to divide physical reality into a class of mutually exclusive and jointly exhaustive entities. What sort of entities could these substances be, given our current state of scientific knowledge? Here is a list of possible candidates:

1. Organisms
2. Artifacts
3. Groups of organisms
4. Elementary particles
5. The cosmos as a whole

I will argue that only the first member of this list, the class of organisms, qualifies. Given the Tiling Constraint, this means that we must find a sixth candidate, a class of entities that is both limited to and exhausts the inorganic world.

Organisms as paradigm substances

For Aristotle and Aristotelians, organisms are paradigm cases of substances (see footnote 4 below). A living organism has causal powers and potentialities, like the powers of self-reproduction, sensation (in the case of sentient organisms), and (in the case of human beings) rational deliberation that are wholly irreducible to the powers and processes of their constituent parts, although they do depend causally on having parts that are in good working order.

The integral parts of organisms satisfy the Homonymy Principle.[8] That is, each integral part of the organism is essentially a part of that organism (or one of the same natural kind). A human hand is essentially a part of a human being: a detached "hand" is a *hand* only in an equivocal or homonymous sense. The non-homonymous parts of an organism, such as its molecules, atoms, and sub-atomic particles, are only potential or virtual parts: they exist only as potential products of division or death, and as metaphysically derivative, localized aspects of the powers and potentialities of the whole substance. The powers and potentialities of these virtual parts

---

8   By an 'integral part' of a substance, Aristotelians mean a material part, in an ordinary, common-sense parlance. A hand is an integral part of a body, the top half of a sphere is an integral part of the sphere. A non-integral part of a substance would be a metaphysical constituent, like a substantial or accidental form or a quantity of mass-energy.

are wholly grounded in the substantial organism as a whole (see Author 2014).

Why artifacts and groups are not substantial

Despite Aristotle's occasional use of artifacts like statues or axes as examples of the form/matter composition of substances, Aristotle leans toward the view that internally heterogeneous artifacts are mere heaps of smaller substances and not substances in their own right.[9] Aristotelians have several compelling

---

9   See *Metaphysics* (Aristotle 1952), Book Zeta, chapters 7 (1032a19) and 17 (1041b28–31), and Book Eta, chapter 3 (1043b22-24). See also Thomas Aquinas (1995), Book 7, lesson 17, paragraph 1679 and Book 8, lesson 3, par. 1719. To clarify, Aristotle and Aquinas are merely denying that there are individual substances that are internally heterogeneous and unified by some artificially created form. This does not rule out the possibility of homogeneous substances whose chemical composition is of an artificial type, like wine or vinegar. In my view also, there can be homogeneous thermal substances of artificial chemical composition. (Thanks to an anonymous referee for help on this point.)

reasons for following Aristotle's lead. First, such artifacts have no emergent powers. We can explain what an artifact does entirely in terms of the joint actions and passions of its proper parts.

Second, the existence of an artifact depends on extrinsic facts. Two duplicate rocks could be such that one is an ax, crafted by a human being, and another is not an artifact at all, chipped into an ax-like shape by blind, natural processes. Similarly, the hunk of rock composing Michelangelo's David is intrinsically identical to many chunks of marble unseparated from their homogeneous marble contexts. The only difference is that the David has been isolated spatially from other bits of marble. Thus, artifacts lack per se unity, both synchronic and diachronic.

Third, the identity and persistence of artifacts are subject to vagueness—and, apparently, to arbitrary human stipulation. Does an artifact like a restaurant survive its relocation, or a complete change in ownership and management? A change in name or menu? There seems to be no fact of the matter here: we can simply stipulate what we shall mean by "'the same restaurant'." Such arbitrary stipulations are impermissible in the case of substances.

Fourth, artifacts can be composed of living organisms. One could make a swing by lacing several living vines together. The vines continue to be substances, and so the swing cannot be one, without violating the Tiling Constraint. Moreover, artifacts can be composed of mere absences—like holes or depressions (think of a moat, for example). Concrete substances, in contrast, must have a material substrate.

Social groups, like clubs, teams, or nations, are like artifacts in all three respects and so cannot be substantial.

Why fundamental particles are not substances

What about fundamental particles? Are some of them substances? As we have seen, a substance must have its own per se unity through time, an identity distinct from that of all other substances. In quantum mechanics, elementary particles do not qualify.

In quantum mechanics, particles lose their individual identities as a result of being incorporated into quantum systems. When we have a unified or entangled system, we can say that the system contains in some sense contains *two* particles, and yet there is no distinct identity associated with either particle.

This results in the replacement of classical Maxwell-Boltzmann statistics with Bose-Einstein or Fermi-Dirac statistics. For example, photons can be in one of two spin states: either spin +1 or spin -1. When we have two unrelated photons, classical statistics applies, resulting in four possible states (each with an equal, 25% probability): both photons +1, both photons -1, the first photon +1 and the second -1, and the second +1 and the first -1. However, when two photons fuse into a single, emergent system, the photons lose their individual identities. As a result, Einstein-Bose statistics apply, with three possible states (each with an equal 1/3 probability): two photons +1, two photons -1, and one photon in each state. There is no distinction, in the fused case, between two possible ways for one photon to be +1 and one -1. The individuality of each photon has been absorbed into that of the whole, two-photon system. Something analogous happens in Fermi-Dirac statistics to fermions like electrons and protons.

In relativistic quantum field theory, the challenge to the individuality of particles is even greater, since even the number of particles involved in a system can vary according to one's frame of reference (Clifton and Halvorson 2001, Fraser 2008). The very same system might at the same time consist of two particles relative to one inertial frame and three particles relative to another. Such relativity of existence is incompatible with substantiality, since the fundamental entities define the very framework of reality.

Finally, in all interpretations of quantum mechanics except Bohmian mechanics, particles lack definite position most of the time and do not follow definite trajectories through space. In fact, Malament and Halvorson and Clifton show that in relativistic quantum theory, every particle has a finite probability of being located anywhere in the universe at any time (Malament 1996, Clifton and Halvorson 2001). As a result, we cannot assign definite active or passive powers to any particle *in isolation.* Only in the context of a measurement event, or within the context of the cosmos as a whole (Simpson 2021a), can such definite powers and physical characteristics be assigned, and even then, only some of them and only momentarily; thanks to the uncertainty principle, we cannot measure non-commuting properties of a particle at the same time.[10] As noted by Teller (1986), Healey (1991), Silberstein and McGeever (1999, pp. 186–90), Kronz and Tiehen (2002, pp. 325–330), along with many others, the quantum state of a pair of entangled particles is irreducibly a state of the pair as such: it does not

10 Similar restrictions apply in the case of one-world no-collapse interpretations, such as the modal interpretation or Bohmian mechanics. In recent work on the Bohmian theory (Esfeld 2017), no particle possesses an active power intrinsically (even properties like spin, mass, and charge are merely contextual)—or, if Bohmian particles do possess intrinsic powers, they must co-manifest their powers as a cosmic whole (Simpson 2021a)—and the Bell-Kochen-Specker theorem places restrictions on the number and type of the intrinsic properties of particles in modal interpretations.

even supervene on the intrinsic properties or spatial distance between the particles (at any point in time). If particles were substances, then explaining the Einstein-Podolsky-Rosen correlations (which violated Bell's inequality) would require super-luminal causation between widely separated particles—effectively, instantaneous action at great distances.

From an Aristotelian point of view, there is good reason to think that the "fundamental" particles of contemporary physics are merely virtual parts of larger substances, which, unlike these particles, have more-or-less definite location and intrinsic characters, and with enduring identities.

Why the whole cosmos is not a single substance

Jonathan Schaffer (2010) has recently argued that there is only one fundamental entity, the whole cosmos. One of his arguments turns on the fact that there are cosmological reasons for supposing that the entire universe constitutes a single, entangled system. Schaffer convincingly argues that this fact disqualifies individual particles from being substantial, and he suggests that it is arbitrary to stop the progress of ontological holism anywhere short of the entire universe.

Aristotelians have at least three reasons for demurring. First, as we have seen, Aristotelians have good reason to take organisms as substances. Organismic powers and processes are irreducible to either the microscopic or the cosmic levels. One can no more explain an organism's sentience in terms of its place in the universe than one can from the interaction of its microscopic parts. If organisms are substances, then the Tiling Constraint rules out the possibility that the cosmos is also a substance.

Second, the Aristotelian account of empirical knowledge, both of sense perception and of scientific induction, requires the causal interaction between sensory and cognitive powers of human beings, on the one hand, and the active and passive causal powers of the entities being investigated, on the other hand. As Nancy Cartwright (1994) has convincingly shown, an adequate account of scientific experimental knowledge requires the causal isolation of the target of the investigation from its environment. Cosmic monism entails that any such isolation is merely apparent. We cannot interact with the whole universe, since we are inextricably part of it.

Third, Schaffer's argument depends on a no-collapse interpretation of quantum mechanics, since collapse events would have the effect of disentangling previously entangled systems. I have argued (Koons 2018b) against the viability of such no-collapse arguments.

Can Schaffer's monism allow for the various proper parts of the universe to be causally isolated from each other, even though all are metaphysically grounded in the nature of the whole? Much depends on how we think of causal powers. If we follow the Neo-Humean project of David Lewis and attempt to reduce causation to counterfactual conditionals, while simultaneously grounding the truth of such conditionals in brute facts about the pattern of instantiation of essentially inert qualities, then cosmic monism could be compatible with approximately isolated causal powers in many cases. However, such a route is unavailable to the Aristotelian, and recent work in metaphysics suggests that it cannot succeed (see Koons and Pickavance, 2017, 95–104 for an overview of objections to the Neo-Humean project).

If we take real causal powers as part of the fundamental structure of the world, with causal powers entailed by the natures of substances, then such real causal powers cannot be detached from their ultimate substantial bearers, and causal isolation of parts of the universe from other parts becomes unattainable for the cosmic monist (see Tahko 2018 and Simpson 2018). In contrast, it was easy to obtain derived causal powers for macroscopic entities in a bottom-up way under the assumption of *microphysicalism*: any spatial arrangement of powerful microscopic entities would give rise to derived powers for the corresponding composite (assuming that there is one). The resulting composite entity would have, as its derived powers, whatever joint dispositions result from the combined action of the microscopic parts.

However, there is no counterpart to this composition-of-agency model for Schaffer's *priority monism*, according to which all fundamental causal powers belong to the universe as a whole. There is no *natural* way to divide the powers of the whole cosmos into derived powers of its proper parts. The best we can do is to look to various counterfactual conditionals: if part x were to act in way F, then part y would act in way G. But that is to abandon the causal-powers ontology that is essential to Aristotelianism.

There is a version of cosmic monism that is compatible with, and even a version of, Aristotelian hylomorphism. In this version of cosmic monism, the whole cosmos determines what natural kinds or essences there are but doesn't directly determine how these kinds are distributed in space and time. If these essences can then be exemplified by substances with definite and finite locations, and if these localized essences determine causal powers that can be effectively isolated from remote factors in the environment, then this Aristotelian monism would permit the kind of experimentation described by Nancy Cartwright. What is crucial is that the powers of individual substances be mediated by the essential natures of those substances and not directly determined by some large-scale facts about the whole universe.

Tiling requires inorganic substances

Thus, the Aristotelian seems to have only one plausible candidate for the role of substance: the living organism. However, the Tiling Constraint requires that the class of substances exhaust all of nature. Organic substances came late to the history of the cosmos. Unless we are willing to embrace Leibniz's somewhat wild speculation and assume that the world is full of living organisms, we must do something about the inorganic world.

In the Aristotelian model, parts of substances are metaphysically dependent on the whole. Applying this to quantum mechanics would result in the supposition that the states and locations of quantum particles are wholly grounded in the natures and states of the organic or inorganic bodies to which they belong (and not vice versa). We could even go so far as to say that quantum particles have only a *virtual existence* until they come to be manifested in interactions between substances. This accords nicely with the fact that quantum particles lack any individual identity.

Quantum mechanics assigns to particles vectors in a state space, with projections of the vectors on various properties corresponding (via Born's rule) with the probability of our observing the particle's exhibiting the property in question. From the perennial perspective, the quantum representation is a representation of a certain active *power* of the whole substance—a power to manifest a particulate part with certain features in interactions with other substances (in this case, the experimenters and their instruments). The Kochen-Specker theorem of quantum mechanics entails that it is impossible to attribute a full range of determinate properties to these merely virtual entities at all times.

Chapter 3
Deriving Hylomorphism from Chemistry and Thermodynamics

3.1 Against Microphysical Reduction

The perennial philosophy depends on denying that sciences like chemistry, thermodynamics, and biology are reducible to particle or field physics, since entities that are *reduced* to other entities cannot be metaphysically fundamental, and it is chemical and biological substances and not particles or fields that are fundamental.

Most philosophers of science assume that one theory can be *reduced* to another if the dynamical laws of the former can be derived from those of the latter under certain constraints or conditions (the so-called "classical" or "Nagelian" model of reduction). However, this common assumption overlooks the fact that every scientific explanation appeals to *two factors*: dynamical laws and a phase space (including a manifold of possible initial conditions). Consequently, every scientific theory comprises two elements: a set of dynamical laws and a space of possible initial conditions. The structure of this space implicitly encodes crucial nomological information.

In order to secure a metaphysical conclusion about dependency between the domains of two theories, it is not enough to derive the dynamical laws of one theory from the dynamical laws of the other, supposedly more fundamental theory. We must also prove that the structure of the phase space and of the manifold of possible initial conditions of the supposedly reducing theory is not itself grounded in the structure or laws of the reduced theory.

Suppose, for example, that we have two theories, T_1 and T_2. Theory T_1 consists in a set of dynamical laws D_1 together with a phase space S_1, and T_2 similarly consists of laws D_2 and space S_2. Let's suppose that we have a Nagelian reduction of T_1 to T_2: a translation * from the vocabulary of T_1 into T_2 such that D_2 entails $(D_1)^*$ with respect to space S_2, but $(D_1)^*$ does not entail D_2 with respect to S_2: that is, the set of trajectories (the flow) through S_2 that are logically consistent with D_2 is a proper subset of the set of trajectories through S2 that are consistent with $(D_1)^*$.

Would this narrow or Nagelian "reduction" give us grounds for taking the entities and properties of T_1 to be wholly *grounded* in those of T_2? Not necessarily: we have to take into account the role of the phase spaces S_1 and S_2. Suppose, for example, that the structure of S_2 (the supposedly reducing theory) is metaphysically grounded in the structure of S_1: it is facts about the natures of the supposedly reduced theory T_1 that explains the structure of the space of possibilities used to construct explanations in terms of theory

T_2. It may be, for example, that the structure of S_1 is "tighter" or more restrictive than the structure of S_2 (under any metaphysically sound translation between the two), and this tighter structure might be inexplicable in terms of D_2, theory T_2's dynamical laws. Space S_1 could have additional *structure*, in the form of new, irreducible properties. In addition, there might be no natural restriction on space S_2 that would close the modal gap between S_1 and S_2. On these hypotheses, the Nagelian reduction of the dynamical laws of T_1 to T_2 would carry no metaphysical implications.

It was easy to overlook this fact, so long as we took for granted the ungrounded and even universal nature of the microscopic or microphysical phase space. In classical mechanics, the space of possible boundary conditions consists in a space each of whose "points" consists in the assignment (with respect to some instant of time) of a specific location, orientation, and velocity to each of a class of micro-particles. As long as we could take for granted that this spatial locatedness and interrelatedness of particles is not metaphysically grounded in any further facts (including macroscopic facts), reduction of macroscopic laws to microscopic dynamical laws was sufficient for asserting the complete grounding of the macroscopic in the microscopic, and therefore for asserting the ungroundedness (fundamentality) of the microphysical domain. However, this ungroundedness of the spatial locations of microscopic particles is precisely what the quantum revolution has called into question. As I will argue in the next section, the phase space of macroscopic objects involves classical properties that cannot be derived from the non-commuting, quantal properties of pure quantum mechanics. The introduction of the thermodynamic or continuum limit introduces new mathematical structure to the phase space of thermodynamics, rendering the metaphysical reduction of thermodynamics to particle physics impossible, even though the dynamic law governing thermodynamics (the Schrödinger equation) is wholly derived from particle physics.

3.2 Beyond Pioneer Quantum Theory: Infinite Systems

In this section I will argue for ontological escalation at two levels of scale: particle physics and thermodynamics (or quantum statistical dynamics). I will posit two kinds of entities, along with two sets of fundamental attributes (including natures or essences): so-called "fundamental" particles (quarks, leptons, etc.) and substances at the level of thermodynamic systems. I will call the latter *thermal substances* for short. Thermal substances have metaphysically fundamental thermodynamic properties, including entropy, temperature, and chemical composition and potential.

In the case of thermal substances, the whole is greater than the sum of its parts—in a very literal sense (as we shall see below). Any collection or heap of fundamental particles has only finitely many degrees of freedom (i.e., the position and momentum of each particle), while thermal substances (corresponding to the kind of systems studied in quantum statistical mechanics) have, independently of how we model them or think about them, *infinitely many* degrees of freedom. This very bold claim is considerably stronger than is actually required for genuine ontological escalation. Although I will defend this strong thesis, there is a weaker position to which I can fall back: namely, that thermal substances do not in fact exhibit infinitely many degrees of freedom but inhabit a space of real physical possibilities that can only be *modeled* in quantum mechanics by means of the introduction of an infinity of degrees of freedom. It may be that this infinity is merely virtual, in the sense that the state of the thermal substance can always be exhaustively described using a finite amount of information. Nonetheless, the distinction between those systems that can and those that cannot be modeled successfully by finite quantum models marks a real, ontological difference between those systems (that is, between mere heaps of quantum particles and true thermal substances).

The commitment to an infinite number of degrees of freedom is compatible with the Aristotelian thesis that all infinities are merely potential and not actual. To ascribe a degree of freedom to a system is to describe that system's potentialities. Aristotle was committed to the real *continuity* of matter (see Brentano 1988), which entails an infinite number of degrees of freedom, since each of the *potentially* infinite number of material parts of the continuous body *could* take on accidental property (like velocity or chemical composition) distinct from the corresponding property of the body's remainder. It is important to distinguish two senses of potential infinity: (1) there are an infinite number of different ways in which a substance can be finitely decomposed, and (2) the substance can be decomposed into an infinite number of parts. Aristotle accepts the first and rejects the second. Similarly, we can postulate that thermal substances have an infinite number of degrees of freedom while insisting that any actual state of the system can be exhaustively described with a finite amount of information. The infinity of the degrees of freedom simply represents an infinite number of alternative, potential states of the substance.

This infinite inflation of the degrees of

freedom would have been extremely implausible in *classical* statistical mechanics, where we know that there can be, in any actual system, only finitely many degrees of freedom, since the particles (atoms, molecules) survive as discrete, individual entities. In quantum mechanics, individual particles (and finite ensembles of particles, like atoms and molecules) seem to lose their individual identity, merging into a kind of quantum goo or gunk. For the quantum hylomorphist, when particles participate in a thermal substance, the fundamental physical attributes are possessed at the level of the thermal substance as a whole, and only derivatively and dependently by the individual molecules. Hence, there is no absurdity in supposing that the whole has more degrees of freedom (even infinitely more) than are possessed by the individual molecules, treated as an ordinary multitude or heap.

From the 1950's onward, quantum theory moved from what the chemist Hans Primas called "the pioneer period" to that of *generalized* quantum mechanics. Generalized QM moved away from the Hilbert-space representation of quantum systems[11] to that of an algebra, in which both quantum and classical observables could be combined in a single formal representation. The algebras of generalized QM can have non-trivial *cores*, consisting of the classical properties that *commute* with every other property, representing exceptions to the mutual complementarity of the quantum properties.[12] In

11   A Hilbert space is a space with an infinite number of dimensions. The state of the system can be represented by a single unit vector in this space. Each physical parameter (like a particle's position or momentum) is represented by an operator of a certain kind on this space. A vector in the Hilbert space is called an "eigenvector" of a parameter when it is a fixed point of the corresponding operator. To get the probability of a parameter's taking a certain value, we project the system's unit vector onto the corresponding eigenvector. The result is a value between 0 and 1. In the Hilbert-space representation of dynamics, it is not the vector that "moves" in the space: instead, it is the correspondence between physical parameters and operators that evolves over time.

12   The fact that quantum properties (modeled as operators) do not commute with each other or with the classical properties is the formal coun-

practice, this means representing the classical properties of complex systems (like molecules or experimental instruments) as ontologically fundamental, on par with the quantum properties of the smallest particles.

This emergence of non-trivial cores of classical observables comes about quite naturally as we move from finite to infinite models. In applied physics, it is common to take some parameter to infinity: that is, to replace the original model having some finite parameter with a new model in which that parameter takes the value of infinity. For example, in the so-called "thermodynamic" limit, a system containing n molecules and a fixed volume V is replaced by one in which both the number of molecules and the volume go to infinity, while keeping the density n/V constant. As Compagner explains (Compagner 1987), this thermodynamic limit is mathematically equivalent to the *continuum limit*: keeping the volume constant and letting the number of molecules go to infinity, while the size of each

terpart of Heisenberg's uncertainty principle and of Bohr's complementarity principle.

molecule shrinks to zero.[13] In many applications, such as the understanding of capillary action or the formation of droplets, the continuum limit is the right way to conceptualize the problem, since infinite volumes have no external surfaces and cannot interact with their containers.

There are three reasons for taking infinite limits in physics: (1) for mathematical convenience, (2) in order to isolate some factors from others, and (3) in order to introduce new structure into the representation. The continuum limit in generalized quantum mechanics is an example of the third reason. In 1931, John von Neumann and Marshall Stone proved that finite systems admit of only one irreducible Hilbert-space

---

13 Compagner has in mind the Aristotelian conception of the *continuum* (as discussed in Brentano 1988) rather than the mathematical conception developed by Karl Weierstrass and Richard Dedekind in the nineteenth century. An Aristotelian continuum is simply a body that lacks actual internal boundaries, which will certainly be true of the collection of molecules at the continuum limit, since molecules with zero volume do not have finite surfaces.

representation (von Neumann 1931).[14] Infinite systems, in contrast, admit of infinitely many in-equivalent Hilbert-space representations.[15]

14 An algebraic representation is *irreducible* if and only if it does not have any proper sub-represen-tations that are closed under the relevant func-tions. Stone and von Neumann proved that any two irreducible groups of the appropriate kind (one-parameter unitary groups) are *unitarily equivalent*. Two representations or groups are unitarily equivalent when there is a unitary trans-formation of one into the other (a transforma-tion involving a *unitary*—that is, a linear, bounded, and surjective—operator). In this case, the two representations can be treated as simply two different ways of representing the same physical situation, analogous to the way that changes in units of measurement or the location of the axes of space produce physically equiva-lent representations.

15 As Kronz and Lupher (2005, 1242–43) point out, an infinite system is one that has infinitely many particles or sub-systems, resulting in a *non-separable* Hilbert space. (A separable space has a countable "dense" subset: a set that contains at least one element of every nonempty open sub-set of the space.) It is necessary but not sufficient for the system to have infinitely many degrees of freedom.

This apparent embarrassment of riches in the infinite case turns out to be crucial for the representation of phase transitions, entropy, and thermodynamic phenomena. As Geoffrey Sewell explains:

> "For infinite systems, the algebraic picture [with its infinite number of subsystems] is richer than that provided by any irreducible [single Hilbert-space] representation of observables.... Furthermore, the wealth of inequivalent representations of the observables permits a natural classification of the states in both microscopic and macroscopic terms. To be specific, the vectors in a [single Hilbert] representation space correspond to states that are macroscopically equivalent but microscopically different, while those carried by different [inequivalent] representations are macroscopically distinct. Hence, the macrostate corresponds to a representation [space] and the

microstate to a vector in the representation space." (Sewell 2002, pp.
4–5)

In addition, by moving to the thermodynamic or *continuum* limit, which involves
treating a system with apparently finitely
many particles as though there were infinitely
many, algebraic QM enabled theorists to introduce *superselection rules*,[16] which could be
used to distinguish the different *phases* of matter that can co-exist under the same conditions (such as gas, liquid, solid,
ferromagnetized, superconducting). I will
argue that the use of the continuum limit can
best be interpreted as representing an ontological difference between two irreducibly macroscopic conditions, providing strong evidence
against microphysicalism.

16 In algebraic QM, a superselection "rule" is actu-
     ally a property of a system that cannot change
     through local, microscopic perturbations. The
     different, mutually incompatible values of this
     quantity are called superselection sectors. Such
     distinct sectors can never be found in quantum
     superpositions, unlike quantum observables.

If these infinite models are to be genuinely explanatory, then the use of the continuum limit has to be justified in ontological terms, and not merely as a useful fiction. We don't have to suppose that there is literally an infinite number (whether countable or uncountable) of infinitesimal molecules (and so, to that extent, the model may indeed be fictional), but we must suppose that the molecules *really cooperate in such a way that they fuse into a dynamic Aristotelian continuum* in space. This means that another kind of ontological fusion (a chemical or thermodynamic fusion) must take place in these cases, distinct from but analogous to the quantum fusion posited by Paul Humphreys. (See Woolley 1988, pp. 58–60, 72–78, and 86 for a defense of this interpretation.) As a result of this thermodynamic fusion, the molecules form a continuous *field* of matter, with literally an infinite number of distinct sub-systems, each sub-system corresponding to a different finite spatial *region* (not to a fictional molecule of zero volume), and each with its corresponding degrees of freedom. This is an account of what a thermal substance really is at each point in time, not an account of how thermal substances are generated in time.[17] Each sub-system is a sub-algebra of the von Neumann algebra for the whole universe: one supported by the classical observable restricted to some spatiotemporal region.

Their fusion into such a material continuum is a different way for the quantum particles to relate to our three-dimensional space: not as discrete, separate units but as a single, cooperating mass, resulting in an entirely new dynamical situation, with a new Hamiltonian function, in violation of the metaphysical requirements of Democritean microphysicalism. This escalation does not require any new fundamental force, but the reorganization of

---

17 Thermal substances are always generated by the destruction of pre-existing thermal substances or organisms. What is really transferred to the new substances in cases of substantial change are parcels of mass-energy, charge, baryon number, and other conserved quantities. My point is that this mass-energy is really distributed continuously in the thermal substance (as the infinite models at the continuum limit represent), with particular particles and molecules as merely potential or virtual parts of the whole.

mass and charge in space alters the frame-work (the boundary conditions) within which the usual forces can act.

I propose that the *substantial form* or *essence* of each thermal substance defines an appropriate *topology* on the corresponding C*-algebra (which represents the potentialities of the substance's *matter*, i.e., its infinitely many subsystems), generating a W*-algebra of observable properties for the whole substance (Primas, 1990a, 248).[18] This W*-algebra is derived from

18 An algebra is a *-algebra if it is closed over an inflection operation * such that $(A^*)^* = A$, $(AB)^* = B^*A^*$, and $(cA)^* = \text{conjugate}(c)A^*$, for all complex numbers c. A *norm-complete* *-algebra includes a mapping (its *norm*) from vector A to nonnegative real number $\|A\|$ such that $\|A^*\| = \|A\|$, $\|cA\| = |c| \times \|A\|$, $\|A\| + \|B\| \geq \|A + B\|$, and $\|A\| \, \|B\| \geq \|AB\|$. A C*-algebra is a norm-complete *-algebra possessing the property that $\|A^*A\| = \|A\|^2$. A W*-algebra or von Neumann algebra is a *-algebra of bounded operators in a Hilbert space H that is closed with respect to the weak operator topology of H. A state on a C*- or W*-algebra is a positive, normalized linear functional. A *representation* of a C*-algebra *A* into a Hilbert space H is a mapping from *A* into the bounded operators of H that preserves the *-

the underlying C*-algebra by a GNS construction, based upon an appropriate reference vector in the thermal substance's Hilbert space (a reference vector that reflects the thermal substance's essence). The Hilbert space represents the microstates within each representation (corresponding to the substance's observable macrostates). When a set of thermal substances interact, the ontic states of each substance correspond one-to-one with a disjoint subset of the extremal, normalized positive linear functionals on that substance's W*-algebra.

Each thermal substance thus corresponds to a set of values for classical (mutually commuting) observables in the quantum algebra, the values representing that substance's essential properties. Since these observables commute, the Kochen-Specker theorem does not apply, and we can suppose that all such

algebraic structure. A *GNS representation* is a representation based on a single vector in H (a so-called "cyclic vector"), from which the whole of H can be generated. The existence and uniqueness of such a representation is established by the Gelfand-Naimark-Segal theorem. (Sewell 2002, 19–20, 27) observables have definite values at all times. The classical observables are represented *by disjoint spaces and not by vectors.* Since the classical observables commute with all the other operators in the quantum algebra, and the microstate of the substance corresponds to an irreducible *representation* of the quantum algebra, it follows that classical observables do not enter into superpositions.[19] Thermal substances are never in superposed states with respect to their *essential* properties (including their thermodynamic properties and chemical composition), although they will have virtual parts that are in superposed states, and they may have quantal properties as accidents. For example, supercooled fluids will have both classical and quantal properties.

There are six phenomena each of which can only be explained (given the current state of the field) in terms of the ontological escalation of the thermal level from the microscopic: (1) the objective irreversibility of time,

19 Thanks to an anonymous *Synthese* reviewer for help on this point.

(2) rigorous definitions of entropy, temperature, and chemical potential, (3) the low entropy of the early universe, (4) spontaneous symmetry breaking, (5) phase transitions, and (6) the persistence of chemical form. I will take up each of these phenomena in turn.

A. *The Irreversibility of Time*

As Ilya Prigogine (1997, 49) explains, the *objective irreversibility of time* is essential to the very idea of observation or measurement, and without observation and measurement, science is of course impossible:

> "If the arrow of time existed only because our human consciousness interfered with a world otherwise ruled by time-symmetrical laws, the very acquisition of knowledge would become paradoxical, since any measure already implies an irreversible process. If we wish to learn anything at all about a time-reversible object, we cannot avoid the irreversible processes involved in measurement, whether at the

level of an apparatus or of our own sensory mechanisms."

R. G. Woolley (1988, 56) argues that true irreversibility is possible only at the continuum limit, when the number of degrees of freedom is infinite:

> "[The work of] Ilya Prigogine and his collaborators ... highlights the fact that irreversible processes in quantum mechanics are only possible in the limit of a continuous spectrum; an immediate consequence of this restriction is that no finite quantum system, for example a molecule or finite collection of N molecules with intermolecular interactions, can show irreversible behavior, and the Second Law of Thermodynamics cannot be applied to such systems."

The continuum limit is needed to ground true thermodynamic irreversibility, as noted by Compagner 1989, 115: "The relative measure in phase space occupied by exceptional microstates vanishes in the continuum limit." Geoffrey Sewell (1986, 30) explains why: "The dynamics of a finite system is quasi-periodic, due to the discreteness of its Hamiltonian."

B. Rigorous Definitions of Chemical and Thermodynamic Concepts

The infinite algebraic models of generalized QM provide, for the first time, the possibility of rigorous and non-arbitrary *definitions of the basic thermodynamic properties* of states of matter (liquid, solid, gas), temperature, and chemical potential (see Sewell 2002).

Contrary to what many philosophers believe, science does *not* suppose that temperature is the mean kinetic energy of molecules! Vemulapalli and Byerly 1999, pp. 28–32 explain:

> "If the system is not at equilibrium, temperature is not well-defined, though the mean kinetic energy is…. Temperature is a characteristic of equilibrium distribution and not of either individual molecules

or their kinetic energy. When there is no equilibrium between different kinds of motion (translations, rotations, and vibrations), as in the case of molecular beams, temperature is an artificial construct." (Vemulapalli and Byerly 1999, pp. 31–32; See also Primas 1983, pp. 312–13)

Robert Bishop and Harald Atmanspacher agree:

"Since thermal equilibrium is not defined at the level of [finite] statistical mechanics, temperature is not a mechanical property but, rather, emerges as a novel property at the level of thermodynamics." (Bishop & Atmanspacher 2006, p. 1769)

C. Spontaneous Symmetry Breaking

Quantum thermodynamics and chemistry provide us with examples in which the macroscopic features of the system do not *supervene on* and therefore cannot be exhaustively *explained by* the microphysical facts. That is, we could have two situations that are microphysically indistinguishable and yet chemically and thermodynamically different. Consequently, these chemical differences cannot in principle be explained exhaustively at the microphysical level. An adequate science of matter needs to combine bottom-up (material) and top-down (formal) modes of explanation. The result is not a radical form of theoretical pluralism or the disunity of science, since, as quantum thermodynamics demonstrates, we can combine both modes in a single model.

Strocchi (1985) explains that the continuum limit is needed to explain any *spontaneous symmetry breaking* in quantum-mechanical terms:

> "In the past, the description of physical system exhibiting approximate symmetries was reduced to the problem of identifying explicit 'forces' or 'perturbations' responsible for such

asymmetric effects.... The progress of the last years has shown that the above strategy is not only unconvenient (sic) from a practical point of view, since the existence of asymmetric terms complicates the equations of motion and their identification is somewhat arbitrary, but *it is actually unacceptable on general grounds*, because it is often impossible to reduce symmetry breaking effects to asymmetric terms in the Hamiltonian.... The result is that the dynamics must be defined in terms of a symmetric Hamiltonian and that the symmetry breaking is due to a dynamic instability according to which symmetric equations of motion may nevertheless lead to an asymmetric physical description.... As we have seen, *such phenomena are possible only for infinite quantum mechanical systems*." (Strocchi 1985, pp 117–18; emphases mine.)

D. *Entropy of the Early Universe*

We can explain the low entropy of the early universe. Roger Penrose has made the plausible suggestion that it either is a law of nature or follows from some law of nature that the universe began to exist in a state of extremely low entropy. According to Penrose, the odds of such a low state of entropy occurring by chance are in the order of 1 in 10 to the 10 to the 123rd power (a number which, when written out fully, would require more zeros than there are particles in the universe). The only possible scientific explanation and the only possible ground for the objectivity of the arrow of time would be that there is some sort of law of nature requiring the absolute beginning of the universe to be in a state of extreme low entropy. If the observed beginning of our universe were merely a transition from some

> earlier state, then there would be
> no possible explanation for its low-
> entropy state.

Penrose's suggestion is a plausible constraint on the phase space of quantum mechanics that can only be formulated in a natural way on a macroscopic scale, suggesting that the true structure of the space of microscopic possibilities is in fact grounded in a natural constraint on the space of macroscopic possibilities. As we have seen, thermodynamic properties can be given a rigorous definition only in the continuum limit. If entropy enters into the fundamental laws of nature, it must be a fundamental property of natural things, leading directly to the ontological escalation of thermal substances over fundamental particles.

E. Phase Transitions

Phase transitions, such as those between the solid, liquid, gas states, and between conditions before and after the onset of coherent ferromagnetism or superconductivity in metals, require the use of infinite models (models involving the continuum limit): see Liu 1999, Ruetsche 2006, and Bangu 2009. Phase transitions are an important case of spontaneous symmetry breaking. Geoffrey Sewell provides a clear explanation of this:

> "Thus we have a spontaneous symmetry breakdown, as each phase lacks the rotational symmetry of the interactions in the system. This is a situation which typifies a class of phase transitions. We emphasize here that this situation could not be covered by a model of a finite system, since that would admit only one representation of its observables and therefore would not present the phase structure we have just described...."

We have seen in the preceding Sections that the idealization, whereby a macroscopic system is represented as infinite, provides new structures, which form a natural framework for theories of collective phenomena. (Sewell 1986, p. 19, 34)

As Laura Ruetsche has explained recently:

> "Only in the thermodynamic limit
> can one introduce a notion of equi-
> librium that allows what the Gibbs
> notion of equilibrium for finite sys-
> tems disallows: the multiplicity of
> equilibrium states at a finite tem-
> perature implicated in phase struc-
> ture." (Ruetsche 2006, p. 474)

Microphysicalists must insist that the
models of phase transitions and other thermodynamic phenomena are misrepresenta-
tions of the fundamental dynamics: that what
is really going on is nothing more than the
standard interaction of a finite number of
particles according to the Schrödinger equation of pioneer quantum mechanics. In light
of the indispensability of the continuum
model, microphysicalists have only two options: (1) they can deny that any transition
between phases really happens, insisting that
it is merely an illusion generated by situations
whose complexity exceeds our understanding, or (2) they can try to argue that the
infinite model is somehow a useful approximation of what could, in principle, be

explained using a finite, elementary quantum mechanical model.

Leo Kadanoff seems to take the first option, arguing that the different phases of matter are not really there in the world but only in our scientific and folksy models of the world: "Since a phase transition only happens in an infinite system, we cannot say that any phase transitions actually occur in the finite objects that appear in our world." (Kadanoff 2009, p. 10) Kadanoff relies on the fact that the transition from one phase to another is vague: there is no sensible answer as to when exactly a sample of water begins to boil.

The anti-realist response to phase transitions and other cases of spontaneous symmetry comes at a very high price. Surely it borders on a kind of philosophically induced madness to deny that water really comes in a variety of phases—to deny that there is really any difference between liquid water, ice, or water vapor. Even if these phases are not precisely measurable *data*, they are real scientific *phenomena* to be explained (to use Bogen and Woodward's useful data/phenomena distinction—see Bogen and Woodward 1988, see also Bangu 2009, pp. 500–01). The anti-realist must claim more than just that the different phases do not constitute real natural kinds, with relatively simple, uncontrived definitions—they must insist that any distinction is merely fictional or erroneous, since the use of finite QM models excludes the very possibility of the definability (whether natural or unnatural) of these phase differences.

The vagueness of phase transitions that Kadanoff points to might be a purely epistemic one (reflecting our inability to detect the ontologically sharp transitions), or it might be a kind of ontological vagueness in the very nature of things. In either case, vagueness alone should not be sufficient to convince us of either the *unreality* or the *nonfundamentality* of a phenomenon. Paul Mainwood (2006, pp. 238–43) and Jeremy Butterfield (2011, pp. 1123–30) have defended the second alternative, insisting that the continuum-limit model is a mere idealization, adopted for mathematical convenience only. This approach runs up against the hard, mathematical fact of the von Neumann-Stone theorem: finitary models simply do not have enough states to represent the different phases of matter. The microphysical-ist must claim that every physical system can be correctly modeled by such finite systems, while the Aristotelian escalationist insists that some systems cannot be so modeled, because of the existence of real thermal fusion, requiring an infinitistic QM model.[20] Mainwood proposes that a finite system be counted as undergoing a phase transition just in case there are distinct states (separated by a superselection rule) in the corresponding infinite model, but neither he nor Butterfield can explain how a model with only one state can be a good approximation to a model with a great many. Every finite model necessarily represents the situation as one without a real distinction between phases. How, then, can the finite model be literally true of a situation in which a phase

20 Nota bene: this distinction persists, even if the Aristotelian escalationist adopts the fallback position of denying the literal existence of an infinite number of degrees of freedom. The issue in question is this: does the distinction between finite and infinite models reflect a real, ontological difference in the phenomena? The microphysical-ists must answer, No.

transition exists, while the infinite model is supposedly a mere "useful fiction"?[21] It is far more reasonable to suppose that it is the discreteness of the finite number of molecules that is the useful fiction, and the infinite model that represents the sober truth.

As John Earman has put it (2004), 191: "A sound principle of interpretation would seem to be that no effect can be counted as a genuine physical effect if it disappears when the idealizations are removed." Yet this is exactly what Mainwood and Butterfield attempt to do. Phase transitions are genuine physical effects, and yet they disappear once the "idealization" of infinite degrees of freedom is removed. The only way to acknowledge the genuineness of these effects is to deny that the use of infinite models is a mere idealization in the first place.

If we assume that an explanation in terms

---

21 In addition, Mainwood's proposal has the paradoxical conclusion (as he admits) that very small systems (even a single molecule!) could undergo phase transitions, unless the definition is further burdened with an ad hoc stipulation of minimum size.

of a model is successful only if the model faithfully represents the relevant features of the actual phenomenon, then we must conclude that our current scientific explanations of phase transitions are successful only if it is the infinite, continuum-limit model that faithfully represents the facts, requiring exactly the kind of real thermodynamic fusion that I have described. The required introduction of the continuum limit in our models must represent a real ontological break between the microscopic and the macroscopic, a break of exactly the kind posited by ontological escalation.

F. Persistence of Chemical Forms

Infinite models are needed to explain the *persistence of chemical form*. The Schrödinger equation for a finite system of particles is spherically symmetrical. Thus, there is no explanation in the standard Copenhagen interpretation for the emergence and observed persistence of chemical structure, with its breaking of spatial symmetry.

The key datum here is that of molecular stability. We know that complex molecules (including chiral molecules—molecules with distinct left- and right-handed versions) can be stable for millions of years, a conclusion based on both experimental data and theoretical reasoning. Yet, from the point of view of finite, elementary quantum mechanics, any molecular structure, including chirality, should be transient, in the sense that it corresponds to some observable (operator) in the Hilbert space. Pure, finite quantum mechanical algebras have no non-trivial core: for every operator, there is some observable that does not commute with it. Hence, if a chiral molecule undergoes a measurement-like interaction with its environment with respect to one of those non-commuting observables, its chirality (either left- or right-handed) should go immediately into a superposition of the two states (see Amann 1993, 139). Yet we never observe such a thing.

In addition, measurement collapse cannot produce the key features of symmetry breaking (Earman 2004, 180): "in particular, a symmetric vacuum [ground or equilibrium] state cannot be built as a superposition of degenerate,[22] asymmetric vacuum states." "If one tries to think of the different degenerate states as belonging to the same Hilbert space, then these states must lie in different 'super-selection' sectors between which a meaningful superposition is impossible…. By the same token, a measurement collapse of a superposition cannot produce an asymmetric vacuum state from a symmetric one." (p. 185)

Quantum chemists work around this problem in one of two ways. First, they employ "generalized quantum mechanics," in which they simply add classical observables and a non-trivial core to the pure or pioneer quantum mechanical algebra. This is an exact counterpart to Aristotle's form/matter distinction, with the pure QM observables corresponding to the proximate matter and the classical observables to the form.

The second work-around involves taking

22 In quantum mechanics, two states are *degenerate* when they have the same energy but very different wave functions. So, the two forms of handedness (left and right) are degenerate states of a chiral molecule, for example.

the continuum (or, equivalently, the thermo-dynamic limit), which introduces the possibility of unitarily inequivalent representations and superselection sectors. This too acknowledges the reality of *ontological escalation*: the individual particles and electrons merge together into a continuous chemical soup, which is only *potentially and virtually* particulate in nature. The chemical form of the thermal substance is thus an aspect of its Aristotelian form. Chemical form contributes to exactly those functions that substantial form serves in Aristotle's system: it grounds the classification of a thermal substance by means of natural kinds in terms of its chemical composition, it grounds the persistence of a thermal substance as the same substance over time, and it grounds the substance's active and passive powers in its interactions with other substances. Individual molecules should be thought of as integral parts of thermal substances, just as eyes and hands are integral parts of organisms. A hand cannot be a hand except as part of an organism, and a right-handed chiral molecule cannot be right-handed except as part of a thermal substance.

Generalized quantum mechanics attributes both classical (mutually commuting) and quantum properties to objects. The modern quantum theory of molecular structure is a perfect example. The structure of a molecule, that which distinguishes one isomer from another, including right-handed chiral molecules from left-handed ones, depends entirely on the classical properties of precise location applied to atomic nuclei. As Hans Primas put it:

> "Every chemical and molecular-biological system is characterized by the fact that the very same object simultaneously involves both quantal and classical properties in an essential way. A paradigmatic example is a biomolecule with its molecular stability, its photochemical properties, its primary, secondary, and tertiary structure." (Primas 1983, p. 16)

There is, however, a complication, in that some molecules can be treated as pure quantum systems (modeled by pure or finite quantum mechanical models) and others cannot.

In order to explain the difference, quantum chemists look at two factors: the difference in internal energy between the various molecular structures, and the molecule's degree of interaction with its environment, especially the long-wave radiation field that cannot be excluded or screened off. In effect, relatively small molecules can "inherit" or "acquire" classical properties from their environments, despite the fact that they are too small to undergo the sort of thermodynamic fusion observable in larger systems.

The introduction of the environment does not threaten the reality of ontological escalation, since it is only a partially *classical* environment that can induce the quasi-classical properties of the dressed molecule: in order to produce the superselection rules needed to distinguish stable molecular structures, the environment must have infinitely many degrees of freedom, due to its own thermodynamic fusion. (Primas 1980, p. 102–05; Primas 1983, p. 157–59)

As R. F. Hendry points out, a molecule's acquisition of classical properties from its classical environment, thereby breaking its microscopic symmetry, should count as form of "downward causation":

> "This supersystem (molecule plus environment) has the power to break the symmetry of the states of its subsystems without acquiring that power from its subsystems in any obvious way. That looks like downward causation." (Hendry 2006, pp. 215–16)

3.3 Objections

I will consider here four objections: (1) one based on anti-realism about thermodynamic properties and phenomena, (2) the claim that infinite models are mere mathematical conveniences, not to be interpreted realistically, (3) the claim that we can justify infinite models without escalation, by appealing to the infinite number of degrees of freedom in the surrounding electromagnetic field, and (4) the claim that the price of rejecting atomism in favor of a literal continuum of matter is simply too high.

First objection: there simply are no thermodynamic properties, phase transitions, etc. This objection consists in going resolutely anti-realist about thermodynamic phenomena. However, this is to fly in the face of empirical fact, as Bangu has argued:

> The problem is that, on the one hand, it is unquestionable that we witness a physical discontinuity taking place—we all see the condensation of vapors on the wall of the tea kettle every morning; on the other hand, we can't point out the precise moment when the transition occurs. Strictly speaking, then we cannot observe the moment when the physical discontinuity occurs. Hence, insofar as a singularity is supposed to characterize it, a singularity does lack observational significance—while again, this does not preclude the singularity having physical significance…. Thus, singularities do not occur at the level of direct observation (the level of

data) but at the next level up, so to speak, the level of phenomena, which are inferred from the data. (Bangu 2009, 500–01)

In addition, if thermodynamic properties are unreal, then so are chemical properties, including the structure of molecules. We would have to treat all of chemistry as a kind of useful fiction, leaving us with no possible explanation of the endurance of chemical form.

Second, defenders of microphysicalism could argue that infinite models are merely mathematical conveniences. On this view, athough finite quantum-mechanical models lack the formal properties that are needed (including phase transitions and irreversibility), they do provide approximations to the needed features that are good enough for all practical purposes. For example, although processes in finite models are never strictly irreversible, many of them are irreversible within the future lifetime of the cosmos and so "practically irreversible."

Jeremy Butterfield has appealed to the convenience of fractal as an analogy (Butterfield

2011, pp. 1090–1103). Fractals are infinite models, and fractals have properties, in particular, non-integer dimensionality, that finite shapes lack. Nonetheless, fractal geometry is extremely useful in modeling nature. Similarly, microphysicalists have argued that the discontinuities of infinite models are approximated well by steep peaks in finite models. (Menon & Callender 2013, 220. Kadanoff 2013, 163)

However, these suggestions provide no explanation of the shift to new dynamical laws that infinite models enable. In addition, they take the objective arrow of time and the Second Law of thermodynamics for granted, with no hope of an explanation or ground.

Vague appeals to "steepness" won't suffice, as Paul Mainwood has recognized:

> "The theories really do require a genuine singularity; vague appeals to 'steepness' or an 'extreme gradient' will not do. For we can find finite systems with extreme gradients in the relevant thermodynamic variables which do not become a singularity as the thermodynamic

limit is taken: these do not represent phase transitions." (Mainwood 2006, 214)

The Yee-Lang theory, in common with
other treatments, requires a genuine disconti-
nuity, not just an extreme gradient in the free
energy. We can easily construct finite systems
with extreme gradients in their free energy
that do no develop discontinuities when the
thermodynamic limit is taken; these do no signify genuine phase transitions. (Mainwood
2006, 232)

There is a still deeper problem: the finite
models of quantum statistical mechanics presuppose a finite number of molecules, each
with its own chemical structure. These facts
cannot be explained by finite models of
quantum particle theory, because they require spontaneous symmetry breaking,
which, as we have seen, arises only in infinite
models. Thus, attempts to explain the thermodynamic phenomena (like phase transitions) using such finite models are viciously
circular, as Hans Primas recognized (190,
107):

> "I would like to stress that every method whatsoever (e.g., the adiabatic approximation, the generator coordinate method) which is intended to give a description of a molecule in terms of electronic structure and a nuclear framework cannot avoid using a commutative algebra of observables." (Primas 1980, 107)

Any commutative algebra of observables requires superselection rules, and an infinite model (to escape the Stone-von Neumann theorem). Laura Ruetsche summarizes the argument for macrophysical realism:

> "… without the idealizations committed to reach the thermodynamic limit, we lack rigorous mathematical models of macroproperties like magnetization, and the relations into which those properties fall— including the relations constituting critical phenomena and exhibiting universality. Lacking models of critical phenomena in individual

systems, we also lack a collection of models featuring the same critical behavior: we lack any systematic theoretical purchase on universality. Lacking this purchase, we cancel the explanatory agenda of explaining universality. Canceling that agenda, we do away with Renormalization Group theory, an approach whose explanatory bona fides come from advancing that agenda. In short, ... [the] idealizations of the thermodynamic limit are essential for modeling the full range of behavior that falls under the ambit of enormously fruitful Renormalization Group approaches to critical phenomena and universality." (Ruetsche 2011, 339)

Third objection: we can get infinitely many degrees of freedom by coupling with the electromagnetic field in an infinite universe. The microphysicalist could agree with me that the correct models of thermodynamic and chemical phenomena have an infinite number of degrees of freedom but propose that the additional degrees of freedom come not from some hylomorphic transformation of the finite system of molecules but rather from the coupling of the finite system with the universe's electromagnetic field. The total system (molecules plus electromagnetic field) could then have infinitely degrees of freedom, thanks to its inclusion of the field. (See Earman 2004, 192; Emch and Liu 2005)

Alternatively, the microphysicalist could hypothesize that each simple particle has an infinite number of unknown, as yet undiscovered parameters, as Jeremy Butterfield has suggested (Butterfield 2011, 1077). I have three responses to this objection.

First of all, we don't know that the electromagnetic field really does have infinitely many degrees of freedom. In order to avoid the infinite energies resulting from self-interaction, quantum field theorists posit some sort of energy cutoffs, which reduce the number of degrees of freedom of any given field to a finite number.

Second, as noted above (footnote 18), it

is not sufficient for the model to have infinitely many degrees of freedom: it must have infinitely many sub-systems, resulting in a non-separable Hilbert-space representation.

Third, and more importantly, it is not sufficient to simply add an infinite number of extraneous degrees of freedom to our finite models of chemical phenomena. The additional parameters must have some explanatory relevance to the phenomena in question, as Mainwood recognizes (Mainwood 2006, 228). What is essential is that we add infinitely many degrees of freedom by taking the finite system to its continuum or thermodynamic limit. The result perfectly matches Aristotle's hylomorphic model: the finite models represent material causation (constraint from the bottom up), and the continuum limit represents formal causation (constraint from the top down).

Turning now to the fourth objection, the microphysicalist could argue that the cost of abandoning atomism, the ultimately discrete character of matter, is simply too high. However, in the context of quantum mechanics this seems quite wrong. In the quantum world, we're used to accepting a pervasive particle/wave duality. Why not an equally pervasive duality of the dense and the discrete?

The use in QM of Einstein-Bose and Fermi statistics suggests that individual quantum particles lose their determinate identities when fused into a quantum system. If that individual identity of particles can be truly lost, why is it hard to believe that matter in the resulting fusion could act in certain circumstances as though it were continuously and not discretely distributed in space? As an additional analogy, we could look to the matter density version of GRW theory, in which the primitive ontology or "beables" (to use John Bell's term) of the models consist in a continuous distribution of matter. One final analogy is provided by quantum field theory, in which even the number of fundamental particles can be indeterminate—in a state of quantum superposition—and can even vary (in relativistic QFT) depending on one's frame of reference.

Chapter 4

Hylomorphism and the Measurement Problem

In fact, even apart from these considerations about quantum chemistry and thermodynamics, pure quantum theory itself (in the form of Schrödinger or matrix dynamics) indicates the incompleteness of the quantum domain, as recognized by Niels Bohr. The predictions of quantum dynamics all take the form of probabilities, but probabilities of *what*? The standard answer (following Bohr) is: the probability of *measurement results*. But what are measurement, and how do they have definite results? This leads to what is known as the *measurement problem* or *measurement paradox*.

4.1 What is the Measurement Problem?

A quantum measurement consists in an interaction between a human experimenter, various experimental materials (instruments, laboratory setups, and the like), and a source of quantum particles. But macroscopic entities (like experimenters and their instruments) are themselves entirely composed of quantum particles, and so quantum dynamics should apply to them as well. This leads to an infinite regress: probabilities of probabilities of probabilities, ad infinitum.

The famous thought experiment of Schrödinger's cat illustrates the first step of the paradox. If the cat is poised to observe some quantum measurement, and if we treat the cat itself as a quantum system, then the interaction between the cat and the quantum phenomenon (say, an electron that could go either up or down) will yield no definite result. Instead, the electron will begin in a superposed Up/Down state, and the cat will come to be in a superposed Observe-up/

Observe-down state, until we open the box and observe what the cat has actually observed. But the observer of the cat could be treated as yet another quantum system, resulting in an infinite regress.

Aristotelian pluralists deny that macroscopic entities like human experimenters and their instruments can be represented adequately by finite quantum models. Thermal substances have classical, mutually commuting properties, like chemical composition, temperature, and phase of matter, properties that never enter into quantum superpositions. When a quantum power interacts with a thermal substance and produces a change in classical properties, a "measurement" has occurred with a definite result.

I can illustrate the hylomorphic solution to the measurement paradox by introducing the thought-experiment of *Schrödinger's ice cube*. We put an ice cube in a box and attach it to a system that responds to some quantum-level event, an event in a 50/50 superposed state. If the system results in an Up event, the ice cube melted, and if it results in Down event, the ice cube remains frozen. Now the ice cube is entirely composed of proton, neutrons, and electrons, and so it is subject to quantum modeling. However, the ice cube is a thermal substance, and so it has a substantial form that imposes a phase of matter (namely, *solidity*) upon those particles. The distinction between two phases of matter occurs only at the level of *form*—it is not determined by the quantum state of the constituent particles. Consequently, it is impossible for a cube to be in a Frozen/Unfrozen superposed state. Such a state simply does not exist. So, we can define a measurement event to be an event involving non-quantal properties (accidents) of substances. Whenever a quantum system produces such an event, a "measurement" occurs, regardless of whether the substance is an organism or merely a thermal substance (like an ice cube). Consciousness need not be involved, and so we escape idealism. This account, I suggest, is consistent with the contextual wave function collapse model put forward by the physicists Barbara Drossel and George Ellis (Drossel 2015, Drossel and Ellis 2018), and discussed by William Simpson (Simpson 2022).

For the hylomorphist, thermal substances and organisms have definite positions in space at each moment in time, even if none of their quantum components do. Each quantum particle is, except for the moment in which its position is measured, located vaguely everywhere, with a certain, finite probability (Clifton and Halvorson 2001). Thermal substances and organisms, in contrast, have a definite, actual location at each moment. Individual quantum particles are really just momentary accidents of substances, and so the locations of the particles do not fix the location of the substance. When not actualized by measurement, individual quantum particles are merely *powers* of interaction, typically non-localized powers. Congeries of such particles (in which the particles lack individual identities) are virtual parts of the substance. (See Chapter 7 for more details.)

Bohr was right in thinking that quantum mechanics indicates the incompleteness of the quantum world. But he was wrong (at least, as he is commonly interpreted) in thinking that the two domains could be kept separate through a dualism of objects or entities. I speculate that this mistake results from unfamiliarity with the hylomorphic solution, in which congeries of quantum particles act as the virtual proximate *matter* for non-quantal *forms*. We now know that even macroscopic objects can have quantal aspects—e.g., super-conductors and super-cooled fluids, which exemplify exotic behavior thanks to quantum coherence effects. Hylomorphists are not committed to a dichotomous quantum/classical dualism but to a system in which complementary entities (namely, substances and accidents, form and matter) co-exist in mutual dependency.

Prompted by the urging of John Bell (1987), defenders of microphysicalism have sought an alternative strategy for resolving the measurement paradox. These efforts have led to revived interest in Everett's many-worlds interpretation, David Bohm's pilot-wave interpretation, and a family of objective bottom-up collapse theories, including the Ghirardi-Rimini-Weber (GRW) theory.[23]

23 The Drossel-Ellis account, like GRW, involves objective quantum collapses, but in their account the collapses are precipitated in a top-down fashion by thermal properties of the system.

These various microphysicalist reactions to the paradox explain why we have a multiplicity of "interpretations" of quantum theory. There was no such plurality of ontological interpretations of Newton and Maxwell—those theories seemed to point clearly to the truth of microphysicalism. Quantum theory no longer does so. Saving microphysicalism requires ad hoc supplementation.

Now, no one can be forced by quantum mechanics to embrace hylomorphism. Nonetheless, the hylomorphic rejection of microphysicalism preserves the simplest and most natural interpretation of the quantum formalism. It is well-supported by the use of the thermodynamic limit in chemistry and thermodynamics, as required by the Stone-von-Neumann theorem. Unlike the other interpretations, hylomorphism does not require any ad hoc modifications or unverifiable additions, and it accords best with the actual practice of scientists. Practicing quantum scientists, like everyone else, are implicit Aristotelians, as the philosopher of science Nancy Cartwright (1994, 1999) has argued since the 1990s.

The different responses to the measurement problem produced the different "interpretations" of the formalisms of Pioneer Quantum Mechanics. Here are the five most common and well-defended interpretations:

1. The Copenhagen interpretation or family of interpretations, comprising a variety of pragmatic, operationalist, perspectivalist, and anti-realist interpretations, including that of Niels Bohr. Quantum states are defined in terms of experimental results and have no independent existence.

2. Dualist interpretations: Eugene Wigner, John von Neumann. Human consciousness causes a "collapse of the wave packet": a discrete transition from a superposed quantum state into a state in which the system possesses some definite value of the appropriate classical property (position, momentum, etc.). This involves positing two distinct dynamics in the world—one occurring autonomously, the other existing in response to interactions with consciousness.

3. David Bohm's interpretation (Bohm

1951), building on Louis de Broglie's 1925 pilot wave account. The pure quantum world exists with a unified, uninterrupted dynamics. The universe consists of point particles with definite locations at all times, guided by the wave function, and forming a single, indivisible and non-localizable dynamical system.

4. Hugh Everett's (1957) "relative state" or "many worlds" interpretation, developed by Bryce De Witt, R. Neill Graham, David Deutsch, and David Wallace (Wallace 2008). The classical world of experiments is merely an appearance, a product of the limited perspective of human and other organisms. When performing experiments involving interaction with systems in superposed quantum states, the observer splits into multiple versions, one corresponding to each possible state. Each split state involves no awareness or memory of states experienced in parallel branches.

5. Objective collapse theories, such as GRW (Ghirardi et al. 1985). These interpretations are like the dualist versions, except

that the collapse of the wave packet is triggered by certain physical events and not by consciousness. At this point, these theories go beyond interpretation, postulating a new, so-far merely speculative collapse-triggering mechanism. At this point, there is no specific theory and no empirical confirmation. In addition, objective collapse theories require still further ontological interpretation, such as John Bell's "flash ontology" (Bell 1987) or the matter density model.

Hylomorphism with its power ontology can be offered as a sixth interpretation, an interpretation inspired by some remarks of Heisenberg (1958) and defended by Nancy Cartwright (1999) and Hans Primas. Interaction between the quantum powers of one substance and the substances making up the experimenters and their instruments precipitates an objective collapse of the quantum object's wavefunction, as a result of the joint exercise of the relevant causal powers of the object and the classical instruments, and not because of the involvement of human consciousness.

Hylomorphism and the Measurement Problem

How is this a solution to the measurement problem? Why haven't I merely re-stated the problem by referring to "observers" and their "classical instruments"? My answer is this: according to hylomorphism, observers and their instruments are substances (or made of substances), and substances are not composed of quantum particles. The states of substances are not reducible to the quantum states of their particles. Thus, there is no inconsistency in supposing that substances have properties ("classical") that are exempt from superposition and that, therefore, always constitute definite outcomes. I will explain how this works in more detail in section 7.2 below, following the work of Hans Primas.

Do we need perennial philosophy and not just some version of contemporary powers ontology? Yes, because if we try to solve the measurement problem with powers alone, we will have to attribute those powers to quantum particles and only to quantum particles. This would include both active and passive powers. Solving the measurement problem requires observers and their instruments to have *non-quantal passive powers*, through which they can register definite results and not merely enter into an extended superpositions. As I have argued in Chapter 3, Aristotelian substances have the capacity to bear irreducible chemical and thermodynamic properties (as represented in the nontrivial centers of infinite algebraic models). Quantum particles do not have that capacity: they are fully characterized by vectors in a single Hilbert space in a finite algebra with only a trivial center and no superselection sectors.

4.2 Epistemological Constraints on a Solution to the Measurement Problem

To solve the measurement problem, it is not enough for an interpretation of quantum mechanics to merely *save the phenomena*, in the sense of merely explaining how it is possible for us to experience the appearance of a macroscopic world (with objects instantiating mutually commuting, *classical* observables like actual position). We must distinguish between *explaining* and *explaining away*. A credible scientific theory must explain most of our apparent data, in the sense of both treating it as objectively known fact and providing a satisfactory causal account of its genesis. A scientific theory that *explains* the data by entailing that it is all a mere appearance, without objective reality, destroys its own empirical foundations.

More specifically, here are some epistemological constraints that must be satisfied (see Simpson 2020, Chapter 8, and Simpson, 2021b):

E1. Perception. The theory must endorse the fact that our sensory perception of physical events and objects is mostly reliable.

E2. Memory. The theory must endorse the fact that our memory of past observations is mostly reliable.

E3. Induction. The theory must endorse the fact that the physical events and facts that we observe (currently and in memory) are an inductively reliable sample of the whole.

As we shall see, each of the new interpretations of QM fails one or more of these tests, in contrast to the power ontology of hylomorphism.

The non-locality of quantum mechanics, as exemplified by Bell's theorem, threatens condition E1. If we embrace a Neo-Humean account of causation, the immediate consequence is that causation in the quantum domain is radically non-local. By *radically non-local*, I mean that the intensity of the influence of distant bodies does not decrease as distance increases. Very remote objects (if entangled with something in our neighborhood) can have effects every bit as significant as other objects in that same neighborhood. In principle, at least, this raises questions about the reliability of our sensory perception of our immediate environment, since our brains or our sense organs might be entangled with distant objects in a way that makes them unreliable as indicators of local conditions.

Hylomorphists can secure the justifiability of reliance on perception by positing receptive causal powers that, when not interfered with by abnormal conditions (whether internal or external), actualize themselves in the form of veridical impressions of one's environment. Since Neo-Humeans lose such a robust Aristotelian theory of causal powers, with its distinction between normal and abnormal conditions, they are left with a situation in which the fallibility of the sensory process makes it unreasonable to treat any sensory impression as knowledge-conferring.

4.3 The Neo-Copenhagen (Hylomorphic) Program

The old Copenhagen view of Niels Bohr suffered from being too narrowly dualistic, distinguishing the classical world from the quantum world. In contrast, the hylomorphic interpretation embraces a salutary kind of ontological pluralism, recognizing that the non-quantum or supra-quantum world is itself a "dappled" world (as Nancy Cartwright puts it), dividing naturally into multiple domains at multiple scales. This fits the actual practice of scientists well, who are in practice ontological pluralists, as Cartwright has documented.

The measurement problem arises from the formulation of quantum mechanics as a theory about the probabilities of certain measurement results. The quantum wavefunction evolves in a deterministic manner, by the unitary dynamics of Schrödinger's equation. In order to test the theory, some observable results must be deduced from the theory. It is Born's rule that enables us to move from some parameter value in the wavefunction (the wave amplitude) to something testable: namely, certain probabilities about the result of measuring one or other classical parameter (such as position or momentum). This early model (as developed by Bohr and Heisenberg) assumed that we could continue to use classical language in describing the experimental setup and the measurement devices. Critics have argued that this involves an implicit inconsistency, since physicists assume that these classical instruments are wholly composed of quantum systems and so should be, in principle, describable in purely quantum and not classical terms.

This charge of inconsistency falls flat when lodged against the hylomorphic version of the Copenhagen program. Observers and their instruments are not reducible to their quantum constituents—instead, quantum particles have only virtual existence, corresponding to certain powers of thermochemical substances. Theoretically, this depends (as I showed in the last section) on the use of algebraic formulations of quantum mechanics with infinite models (at the continuum limit). The additional structure afforded by such models represents the irreducible fundamentality of these substances.

Bohr's interpretation required that reality be divided into two disjoint realms, the classical and the quantum, with a measurement involving any setup in which a quantum system is made to act upon a classical observer or instrument. This foundered on the fact that some systems, like supercooled fluids or quantum computer chips, bridge the gap between the two realms. We cannot consistently describe all macroscopic objects in purely classical terms, as Bohr's program seems to require, since it is interaction with the classically described realm of measurement devices that collapses the wavefunction in Bohr's model. In contrast, on the Primas model, we could postulate that the wave packet associated with a quantal property has "collapsed" whenever it becomes correlated with a fundamental *classical property* of a disjoint system. Even though entities cannot be neatly divided into two disjoint domains, this is not true of physical properties. Substances have *both* classical properties *and* (by virtue of their virtual parts) quantal properties. Infinite algebraic models represent quantal properties as vectors in individual spaces and classical properties as disjoint spaces or superselection sectors.

Primas demonstrates (Primas 1990b) that interaction with the classical properties of entities in the environment will drive quantal vectors to eigenstates with a high probability in a short period of time. The Primas solution is, consequently, one of continuous rather than discrete collapse (unlike, for example, most versions of the GRW model of objective collapse). The Primas model can be incorporated into a powers ontology, by attributing to substances the power to collapse the wavefunctions associated with quantum parts of other substances.

Bell characterized the measurement succinctly in this way: either the Schrödinger equation isn't right, or it isn't everything. Most solutions to the problem fall squarely into one side or the other: the Copenhagen interpretation and the many-worlds interpretation insist that the equation isn't everything, while the GRW and other objective collapse theories suppose that it isn't right. On which side does hylomorphism stand? I've described it as a neo-Copenhagen view, while Primas offers a model of objective collapse.

Of course, Bell's alternatives are not exclusive. In fact, the Schrödinger equation is neither everything nor right. It is right insofar as it describes the evolution of the quantal aspects of a substance sans interaction with other substances. However, this is not everything, since thermal substances also possess determinate, non-quantal properties. And it is incorrect, even as a description of those quantal aspects, whenever the quantum potentialities are actualized through interaction with other substances. At that point, a form of objective collapse takes place, in a way described by Primas's model.

4.4 The Bohmian Program

Like the Bohm view, the hylomorphic interpretation assumes a broadly realist stance toward the classical world. Bohm takes classical objects to be composed of particles really located (for the most part) in the regions of space that they appear to occupy in our experience. A deterministic version of Bohm's theory would seem to offer Neo-Humeans and microphysicalists their best chance at surviving the quantum revolution. Each particle in Bohm's theory has a definite location at each time, and these locational states are indeed fully separable. Each particle has its own unique identity, blocking any quantum fusion.

However, there are real concerns about whether Bohm's theory can underwrite the reliability of our perception of the positional states of our measuring devices. Our subjective impressions would seem to depend on the contemporaneous states of our brains, not the positions of particles in our measuring devices (or even our sense organs, like the retina). Bohm's theory is certainly capable of generating false sense impressions and false memories about particle positions, since particles do not influence each other's positions, but are always guided by the cosmic wavefunction.

Here's the form of the argument:

1. To be empirically adequate, Bohm's theory must give an account, not just of the "pointer settings" of measuring instruments, but also of our perceptions of those settings (as Bohm himself admitted, [Bohm 1951, p. 583]).

2. There is good reason to think that mental states aren't determined by particle positions within the brain alone. We must include all of the functional features of the brain.

3. But this requires that the basis of mental states includes the state of the cosmic wavefunction, which leads to the radical non-locality of the relevant brain state.

4. In the absence of pervasive and stable decoherence linking brain states and sensible objects, functional states of those states in relation to the brain do not fix particle positions (in either the object or the brain): two pairs of brain-object relational states

can be functionally indistinguishable, even though they involve radically different particle positions and trajectories. Therefore, in the absence of effective decoherence, one and the same system (e.g., the person's brain plus his sense organs) cannot be reliable both at tracking functional states and at tracking particle positions.

5. Non-local quantum effects threaten to destroy any reliable correlation between the functional states of the environment and local particle positions and therefore to destroy any correlation between brain states and particle positions.

6. This could be avoided only if we had good grounds for assuming that environmental interaction secured (through decoherence) the effective classicality of the brain-environment interaction, but that is very much in dispute. In addition, Bohm's theory raises special technical problems for the widespread application of decoherence (see Schlosshauer 2005, p. 1297–98 and Simpson 2021b).

7. Evolution would explain our ability to

track reliably the relevant *functional aspects* of our environment, not our ability to track particle positions. Evolution cares about whether we can survive and reproduce—it is completely indifferent to whether we can reliably track particle positions.

Brown and Wallace explain why the perceptual state must be fixed by the functional state of the brain, not just by its configuration of particles (premise 2):

Observables in the context of Bell's remark are defined relative to sentient observers, and it is a tenet of the de Broglie-Bohm picture that such observers are aware of corpuscles in a way that fails to hold for wavefunctions. Of course, there is an obvious sense in which the corpuscles are also "hidden," and Dürr et al. emphasized in 1993 (Dürr et al. 1993) that the only time we can have sure knowledge of the configuration of corpuscles is "when we ourselves are part of the system." But how exactly is this supposed to work? Stone correctly pointed out in 1994 (Stone 1994) that this claim "certainly fails if our knowledge is based on measurements which one part of our brain makes on another...." (Brown and Wallace 2005, p. 534)

In support of premise 5 (the lack of a simple correlation between brain states and particle positions), Brown and Wallace point out:

> "Suppose we accept that it is the [particle positions] that determine the outcome of the measurement. Is it trivial that the observer will confirm this result when he or she 'looks at the apparatus'? No, though one reason for the nontriviality of the issue has only become clear relatively recently. The striking discovery in 1992 of the possibility (in principle) of 'fooling' a detector in de Broglie–Bohm theory (Englert et al. 2992, Dewdney et al. 1993, Hiley et al. 2000, Brown et al. 1995) should warn us that it cannot be a mere definitional matter within the theory that the perceived measurement result corresponds to the 'outcome'

selected by the hidden corpuscles"
(Brown and Wallace 2005, p. 523).

As premise 6 indicates, Bohmians might respond to this problem by appealing the theory of decoherence. Decoherence involves considering how the action of two systems (thought of as the measuring apparatus and the object under study) on the wider environment can enable them to become approximately classical in their relation to each other, in such a way that they can be assigned stable properties (such as location) that evolve in roughly the way prescribed by classical, pre-quantum physics.

However, it is not at all clear that decoherence will work in the intended way in a Bohmian setting. Sanz and Borondo (2003) studied the double-slit experiment in the framework of Bohmian mechanics and in the presence of decoherence and showed that even when coherence is fully lost, and thus interference is absent, nonlocal quantum correlations remain that influence the dynamics of the particles in the Bohm theory, demonstrating that in this example decoherence does not suffice to achieve the classical limit in Bohmian mechanics. See also Schlosshauer 2005, p. 1298.

Is this problem of perceiving *pointer settings* any greater for the Bohmians than it was in classical, Newton-Maxwell physics? Yes, it is, precisely because of the radically non-local character of Bohmian dynamics. All distant bodies in Newtonian mechanics have a negligible influence on local phenomena, an influence that decreases proportionally to the square of the distance. This is not the case in Bohmian mechanics. There is, therefore, real grounds for doubting whether we can reliably detect the actual positions of Bohmian particles, contrary to principle $E1$.

4.5 The GRW/Objective Collapse Program

The hylomorphic interpretations of quantum mechanics have several advantages over GRW and other non-hylomorphic objective collapse theories. First, hylomorphism does not require speculation about some as-yet-unknown mechanism by which quantum waves collapse into precise states. Consequently, hylomorphists can give a much simpler account of the internal dynamics of the quantum world: the quantum world proceeds without exception according to the dynamics of the Schrödinger equation. Instead of postulating some unknown quantum trigger of wave collapse events, the hylomorphic pluralist simply relies on our actual practice of using instruments with classical features to precipitate precise measurement events. For hylomorphic pluralists, to learn more about how quantum waves collapse is simply to learn more about macroscopic and mesoscopic systems themselves—to learn more chemistry and thermodynamics and biology. This is in fact the direction taken by generalized quantum mechanics (as I described in Section 5).

In addition, the hylomorphist can take the objects of the "mesoscopic" world (including molecules and cellular structures) as persisting in stable states through time, while the objective collapse view has to be combined with a further account of the ontology of the macroscopic world. For example, if the GRW theory combined with John Bell's "flash ontology" (Bell 1987, Maudlin 2011, pp. 23–57]), in which the macroscopic world consists of a number of widely separated and intermittent "flashes" (like the blinking of a swarm of fireflies), with each flash representing a wavepacket collapse. However, the Bell flash ontology can only provide a relatively small number of "flashes" of determinacy, too small a number to ground the existence of stable molecules and organisms.

The alternative version of GRW theory is the matter density interpretation. In this view, objective collapses result in relatively dense concentrations of expected mass in spacetime regions that resemble the objects of our classical world. The matter density interpretation shares with Bohmian theory the problem of verifying the reliability of our sense perception, and for similar reasons (both theories involve a high degree of causal non-locality). As Schlosshauer has pointed out, decoherence is of relatively little help to objective collapse theories [67, pp. 1293–96].

In addition, as Alexander Pruss has recently argued (Pruss 2015a), non-hylomorphic objective collapse theories face a problem with respect to the epistemological constraint E2, the reliability of memory. GRW is not really a single theory but a family of theories. The family has a single free parameter, which we can call (following Pruss) f, the *hitting frequency*. The hitting frequency gives us the probability of the collapse of any system of entangled particles, as a function of the total mass of those particles. We can put an upper bound on the hitting frequency—if f were too high, then we would never observe the kind of entanglement that is characteristic of the quantum realm. However, this experimental data puts no lower bound on the f. The frequency could be so low that it is very unlikely that any system should ever collapse. The argument against such a low frequency has to be philosophical and phenomenological rather than scientific: if the frequency were that low, human observations would never have definite or delimited outcomes, contrary to our experience.

Pruss suggests that we take such low frequencies seriously:

"But imagine f is so low that typically a collapse in something the size of my immediate environment occurs only every hour. On its face this is ruled out by my memory of the past five minutes. But suppose, as seems reasonable on GRW, that consciousness occurs only when there is no superposition of brain states that constitute consciousness. Nonetheless, even when consciousness does not occur, my brain states will be evolving in superposition, and when they collapse they will give rise to conscious false memories of having had conscious states over the past period of time. We thus have no way of empirically ruling out such low values of f."

In other words, the proponents of GRW can rule out such low hitting frequencies by assuming (without argument) that our memories are veridical. However, the GRW family of theories, if true, would give us good reason to doubt that veridicality. If GRW were true and the hitting frequency were low, my *present experience* would be exactly the same. I could know that I have just now experienced a collapse of the wave function, but I could not have any confidence that any of my apparent memories of precise observations in the past are veridical. It isn't just that proponents of GRW are, like all of us, subject to Cartesian doubts. It's rather that the GRW program provides positive support to the skeptic's worries. If the hitting frequency is low enough, my memories are radically unreliable as manifestations of the actual past. Some degree of reliability is a condition of knowledge.

The defenders of GRW might object to this reduction to skepticism by arguing that it is legitimate for them to take into account the need to secure the reliability of our memory in fixing the value of the hitting frequency parameter. Why can't they simply build a sufficiently high hitting frequency into their theory as a way of blocking the argument for skepticism?

I have two responses. First, since *f* is a free

parameter of the theory, the only legitimate way to settle its value is empirically. However, its value cannot be settled empirically without presuming (at least implicitly) that our memories are indeed reliable. Hence, it would be viciously circular to set the frequency high enough to ensure the reliability of our memory. In contrast, the hylomorphist treats the reliability of our memory as a fundamental fact about the human form, with no free parameters whose value-determination requires empirical input.

Second, the GRW theorist is vulnerable to epistemic defeat, along the lines developed by Alvin Plantinga (1993, 2002, 2011). In the absence of any physical or metaphysical constraints on the value of f, we have to take seriously the possibility that the value of f might be extremely low. We know that our memory is very unreliable, on the assumption that f is low (most of our apparent memories are illusory). In that situation, we cannot appeal to our memory of the past to verify the reliability of our memory without obvious vicious circularity. Thus, we cannot justify continued rational belief in the reliability of our memory, given the real possibility of an undercutting defeater which cannot itself be defeated.

In contrast, there is no similar consideration forcing the hylomorphist to recognize any possibility of the unreliability of our powers of memory.

Finally, even if we were to grant that the hitting frequency is so low that such false memories would be extremely unlikely, this is not sufficient for our memory-based beliefs to constitute knowledge. A very high probability of truth is not sufficient for knowledge, as the famous *lottery paradox* illustrated. I can know that the probability of each ticket's winning is extremely low—in a hypothetical lottery with an astronomical number of tickets, fantastically low. However, such a low probability of falsity is not sufficient to give us knowledge of truth, since if I could know that each ticket is a loser, I could also know that they all are, which in fact I know to be false. What's needed for knowledge is the exercise of some cognitive power which, if exercised in normal circumstances and without external interference, guarantees absolutely the truth of the belief formed. Given GRW without hylomorphic powers, our memory-based beliefs can never meet that standard.

Therefore, GRW theories and other objective collapse theories fail epistemological constraint E2.

GRW theories also fail constraint E1, perception, for reasons noted by David Albert and Lev Vaidman (Albert 2015, Albert and Vaidman 1989). The human visual system is quite sensitive to small numbers of photons—as few as six or seven suffice. However, such a small collection of photons has a vanishingly small probability of inducing a wave-function collapse under GRW models. Aicardi et al. (Aicardi et al. 1991) responded by arguing that the movements of ions in the human nervous systems that correspond to the apparent perception of photons is sufficient to guarantee a collapse with high probability within the time frame of conscious perception. However, this is not sufficient to satisfy E1, since it means that almost all of our visual perceptions are factually inaccurate. They represent events occurring in our environment, events that are ontologically independent of the movement of ions in our optic nerves and brains. If GRW is correct, however, that what we see when we see something is actually an event occurring within our own nervous systems. There was no corresponding external event consisting of the emission of a localized photon that we were able to detect. Once again, GRW can *save the phenomena* but only at the expense of undermining human knowledge.

4.6 Conclusion

Aristotelianism provides us with a metaphysical framework that is sufficiently flexible to accommodate fundamental modes of causation at the level of thermodynamics, chemistry, and solid-state physics. By doing so, we can circumvent the usual measurement problem, which presupposes that an exhaustive description of the world at a fundamental level can be given in terms of pioneer quantum mechanics, with no non-trivial center of classical properties.

Additional work needs to be done in exploring the relationship between a purely quantal description of particles (taken either individually or as definite pluralities of discrete entities) and the metaphysically more fundamental level of substances and their causal powers. In particular, should we assume that there is a quantum wavefunction that embraces all the particles of the world, simultaneously characterizing the quantum potentialities of all substances, or should we suppose instead that quantum wavefunctions are always local and contingent affairs, part of what Nancy Cartwright has described as a *dappled world*? (Cartwright 1999) The hylomorphic view can be developed in either direction. If we assume a global wavefunction, then we get the *traveling forms* interpretation of Alexander Pruss (Pruss 2018), in which substantial forms of interacting substances induce global collapses of the wavefunction. I will introduce the traveling forms model in the next chapter. The dappled world alternative has been developed by William Simpson in his dissertation (Simpson 2020), and it is that model that is tacitly presupposed by Primas's model of collapse. It also underlies recent work by Barbara Drossel and George Ellis. (Drossel and Ellis 2018)

This issue corresponds to a further question about the extent of entanglement in nature. The global wavefunction picture would suggest that entanglement is pervasive in nature, arising with the Big Bang and never fully disappearing. On the dappled world picture, entanglement occurs only under special circumstances, when complex systems are prepared in a way that is isolated from the surrounding environment. Local collapses destroy these fragile entanglements.

Chapter 5
The Many-Worlds
Interpretation of
Quantum Mechanics

5.1 Introduction

The so-called Many Worlds Interpretation of quantum mechanics has been extant now for nearly sixty years, beginning as H. Everett III's doctoral dissertation in 1957 (Everett 1957), with further contributions by B. DeWitt and N. Graham in their 1973 book, *The Many Worlds Interpretation of Quantum Mechanics* (DeWitt and Graham 1973). The Everett approach takes quantum mechanics both realistically and as a stand-alone, autonomous theory of the world, not in need of a separate theory of measurement to bridge the apparent gap between the deterministic evolution of the wave-function in a highly abstract, probabilistic space and empirically observable statistics in the laboratory. Instead, Everett proposed that all of the apparently contradictory macroscopic results assigned some finite probability by the theory are equally real, coexisting in distinct sets of relative states. DeWitt and others later identified these clusters of mutually consistent relative states with distinct and co-existing worlds or branches of the world.

These early versions of the interpretation faced a huge problem: there were no worlds or branches, describable in macroscopic terms, to be found in the formalism of quantum mechanics itself. We can find within the formalism something called superpositions, which are states that seem to attribute to particular systems (like particles) a plurality of mutually inconsistent properties, each with a certain amplitude, but there seems to be no way to recover macroscopic instruments and determinate measurement relations from these isolated superpositions. This problem is often described as the problem of finding a *preferred basis*, since the decomposition of the world into discrete branches can only take place relative to a selection of a certain set of parameters. Any selection of such a basis seemed arbitrary and unprincipled, and so the objectivity of the co-existing branches was thrown into doubt. In addition, there is nothing in the wavefunction that corresponds to the persistence or splitting of branches. Probabilities of various states simply fluctuate over time: there is no way to trace where the probability that once belonged to a given state has moved (either as a unified packet or through fission).

In the 1970's, 80's, and 90's, a great deal of theoretical work commenced on the problem of giving a fully quantum-theoretic account of measurement. This work comprises the programs of decoherence of W. Zurek (1982) and H. D. Zeh (1973) and the consistent histories approach of R. Griffiths (1984), R. Omnès (1988), and Gell-Mann and Hartle (1990 and 1993). The decoherence results show that under favorable circumstances a stable, approximately classical domain can be expected to emerge from the quantum-mechanical descriptions of a measuring system, its object, and the surrounding environment (Wallace 2011). What decoherence left unsolved was why we see the emergence of just one such quasi-classical domain when interacting with quantum superpositions. A marriage of decoherence with the Everett interpretation was inevitable, with the Everett interpretation explaining the apparent uniqueness of result as a product of the relativity of our perspective in this or that branch, and the decoherence providing the missing preferred basis and explaining how to extract persistent and apparently "splitting" quasiclassical domains from quantum descriptions.

The consistent histories approach was even closer to the spirit of the Everett interpretation, since it sought to extract approximately classical domains from the quantum function for the entire cosmos, rather than looking at particular instrument-object-environment arrangements. Here again, the two approaches seemed designed to resolve each other's deficiencies: with consistent histories providing the preferred basis, and the Everett interpretation dissolving the worry about what to do about certain regions or phases of the cosmic history in which there are no consistent histories at all. On the Everett interpretation, only the quantum wavefunction describes fundamental reality, so only it can be expected to have universal validity. Consistent histories simply describe the approximate emergence of quasi-classical branches under favorable circumstances including, presumably, our own.

In recent years, the Many Worlds Interpretation has found a new home in Oxford, among both physicists and philosophers of science, including David Deutsch, Simon Saunders, David Wallace, Christopher Timpson, and Harvey Brown. The Oxford group has developed the idea of using decoherence and consistent histories approaches to solve the preferred basis problem, explaining the emergence of approximately classical "domains" from the wavefunction. They have also, building on seminal work by Deutsch (1999), attempted to solve the other central problem of the interpretation, which is that of making sense of the precise probabilities ascribed to different outcomes by applying Born's rule to the wavefunction.

I will argue in this chapter that the Oxford Everettians' attempt to use the philosophical framework of functionalism to elucidate the relation between the manifest world of scientific experiment and observation and the underlying, fundamental quantum reality ends in failure. Specifically, I will identify four failures of this account:

1. I will use Putnam's paradox to demonstrate a radical indeterminacy of content that would afflict all of our scientific theories.
2. I will demonstrate that any consistent story of the world (no matter how fantastic) would count as equally real.
3. As a consequence, it would be impossible for any of our scientific theories to be wrong, making it equally impossible for them to be empirically confirmed.
4. This failure of empirical testability would deprive us of any reason for believing in quantum mechanics in the first place.

I turn in section 5.9 to sketching a neo-Aristotelian alternative to the Oxford Everettian interpretation. This new interpretation adds the additional metaphysical constraints needed to solve the Putnamesque paradoxes in the form of a set of essences of macroscopic substances. This also enables us to use the actualization of these essences as a way of distinguishing the one actual branch from all the merely possible ones. Alex Pruss and I call the resulting interpretation the *traveling branches* interpretation. This interpretation builds on both the realism about the quantum wavefunction and the results of decoherence theory, in exactly the same way as these are treated by the Oxford Everettians, and yet it ends up in a metaphysical and semantic position that is much more defensible.

5.2 Recovering the Manifest Image through Ramseyfication

The central problem for the Many Worlds interpretation is that of bridging the gap between the scientific image of the quantum wavefunction and the "manifest image" (to use Sellars's phrase—Sellars 1962) of our approximately classical, macroscopic world, the world occupied by all experimenters, their instruments, and the results of their experiments. David Wallace's solution is an admirably simple one: all features and entities of the "manifest image" (macroscopic objects, organisms, sensible properties) are to be reduced to *functional roles* realized in some way by the quantum wavefunction—where these functional roles can either be identified with second-order, functional properties, like the property of being water-soluble, or with the quantum-mechanical role-fillers corresponding to those properties (in style of David Lewis (1966, 1972, 1980).

The functional properties can be identified with the result of Ramseyfying (Ramsey 1929) our ordinary folk ontology and our special sciences (including, perhaps, classical mechanics) in the language of pure quantum-mechanics (infinite Hilbert space, unitary Schrödinger evolution). There are three historical precursors to the kind of functionalization of the manifest image that Wallace has in mind: the phenomenalistic project, as typified by John Stuart Mill and the early Carnap, Bertrand Russell's functional-structural account of physics in *The Analysis of Matter* (Russell 1927), and the late-twentieth-century, behaviorism-inspired accounts of the mind, especially the Analytic Functionalism of David Lewis (1966, 1972, 1980). The ideal formal machinery for each attempted functional reduction is F. P. Ramsey's account of scientific theories (Ramsey 1929), well explained by Lewis in (Lewis 1966).

In both the phenomenalist project and in Russell's 1927 structuralism, there was a significant epistemological dimension, based on the idea that we have privileged and certain access only to our own conscious states (a kind of Cartesian starting point for knowledge). That epistemological element is much reduced in Lewis's functionalism, and entirely absent from Wallace's project, so I will, at the risk of some anachronism, present all four programs as if they were concerned solely with ontological issues, that is, with identifying the correct "truthmakers" or truth grounds for the reduced theory.

In this chapter, I will use a model-theoretic version of Ramseyfication, in which, instead of introducing second-order variable and quantifiers for the predicates, we simply extend the interpretation function of a given model in order to turn a model of the original, base language into a model of the emergent theory in an appropriately expanded language.

We must also make use of a set of possible worlds, because all versions of functionalism require that we make some reference to the dispositions of things to respond or behavior in specified ways, even if the things never actualize these dispositions. The simplest formal semantics for such dispositions makes use of the subjunctive conditional: if P were true, Q would be true. We can represent the truth of such a subjunctive conditional at the actual world w* by supposing that w is surrounded by a system of spheres of worlds, representing degrees of closeness or similarity of those worlds to w. The subjunctive conditional $(P \square \rightarrow Q)$ is true at w* if Q is true in all of the P worlds that are "closest" to w*.

For the sake of simplicity, I will assume that each of the individuals exists in only one world. Our interpretation function must assign to each constant (proper name) an individual in each world, and to each n-ary predicate, a set of n-tuples of individuals from that world. This will enable us to assign truth-values at each world to all logically complex formulas.

Let's suppose that we start with a model M_{base}, defined for our base language L_{base}, which represents the fundamental level of reality. Now suppose that we extend the language L_{base} to a language $L_{base+emergent}$, by adding constants, function symbols, and predicates that signify an emergent, non-fundamental level of reality. A theory $T_{emergent}$ of this emergent world is realized in our base model M just in case the interpretation function I_{base} for the model can be extended to a new function $I_{realizer}$, defined for $L_{base+emergent}$, such that the resulting model $M_{extended}$ is a model of $T_{emergent}$. In such a case, we can say that the function $I_{realizer}$ is a *realization* of the emergent theory $T_{emergent}$ in the original base model M_{base}. We extend the interpretation function of the original model in order to provide extensions to all the terms and predicates of the emergent theory.

5.3 Classical Phenomenalism, Russell's Structuralism, and Lewis's Functionalism

Using this model-theoretic approach to realization, classical phenomenalism could be seen as postulating that all truths about the existence and characteristics of physical objects are realized by truths about the private and subjective sense-experience that human observers have or would have under specified, counterfactual conditionals. As Mill put it, physical objects are "mere permanent possibilities of perception." So, we start with a base language L_{phen}, which includes terms for subjects of experience, terms for sense-data, predicates that define sense experiences in terms of the locations of sense data in the egocentric spaces of subjects (with properties like up and down, left and right, forward and back) at times in private, egocentric timelines. The language will also include the subjunctive conditional. We will then consider a class of models for this language, consisting of a set of worlds W, a designated actual world w^*, an interpretation function I for evaluating atomic sentences in each world, and a system of concentric spheres S for the interpretation of subjunctive conditionals. For simplicity's sake, I will treat all sense-data and subjects as world-bound individuals (in Lewis's sense), things that each exist in only one "world." We can then select the model $M_{\text{true-phen}}$ that incorporates all the actual truths about actual and counterfactual experiences. The set of formulas true in $M_{\text{true-phen}}$ is the set $TRUE_{\text{phen}}$, the set of all truths expressible in the vocabulary of L_{phen}.

We now enrich the language by adding terms referring to physical objects, which will now be assigned locations and trajectories in a single three-dimensional (public) space, indexed by universal time. Since we still retain the subjunctive conditionals, we can now express conditional relationships between sentences expressed in purely phenomenal terms and sentences expressed in purely physical terms, and between pairs of sentences both of which are purely physical in form, as well as between sentences that mix both vocabularies.

Russell's structuralist program in *The*

Analysis of Matter is exactly isomorphic to the classical phenomenalist program. The only difference is that Russell does not use subjunctive conditionals, as Mill did, but instead speaks of causal relations, both in the phenomenal and in the physical world. However, he does not offer a substantive account in the 1927 book of what causation consists in, so this is a difference we can, at least for the moment, set aside. In addition, of course, instead of speaking about phenomenal sense-data, Russell in 1927 speaks instead about perceptions, which he takes to be events in the brain with which we are immediately acquainted.

In general, there will be many realizations of any theory T_0 in the model $M_{\text{true-phen}}$, and there will be many other theories in the enriched language besides T_0 that are consistent with the set of all phenomenal truths (and which therefore have realizations in $M_{\text{true-phen}}$). In order to cut down the number of theories and realizations, we need some further constraints both on our theory T_0 and on the permissible realizations of that theory. We can accomplish both of these at once simply by restricting the interpretation function. We can then hope to pick out the one true theory of physics that has a unique permissible realization in the model $M_{\text{true-phen}}$.

In the case of both the phenomenalist and Russellian-structuralist program, these constraints consist in the laws of perspective that link geometrical properties described in terms of public four-dimensional spacetime with properties described in terms of egocentric phenomenal space and time. We can put a constraint on any acceptable interpretation function, requiring that when it identifies a physical object in a world with a set of sense data associated with subjects in that world, the interpretation function must assign a shape and size to the physical object that corresponds to the shape and size of each of the corresponding sense-data, with the correspondence relation fixed by the laws of perspective as applied to the physical location assigned to the relevant subject of experience. That is, the physical primary qualities of bodies must correspond to sense-data and subject-locations in such a way that each sense-datum accurately records the shape of the body, as it would appear to a subject at the location to which the subject is assigned.

This is quite a severe constraint—in fact, too severe, since it fails to take into account the existence of illusions and hallucinations. It is reasonable to suppose that only one theory-interpretation pair will maximize the degree of fit between the bodies and the corresponding sense-data, and we can take this pair to give us both the set of truths about the physical world and the corresponding truthmaker in the phenomenal world for each truth.

David Lewis's version of Analytical Functionalism is exactly isomorphic to the phenomenalist or structuralist model sketched in the preceding subsection. The differences are these: first, the base model with which we begin is a model of something like classical physics and chemistry, including facts about overt behavior, sensory-organ stimulations, and neural structures and patterns of firing. The true model of the world $M_{true\text{-}phys}$ yields a set of physicalistically acceptable truths, $TRUE_{phys}$ in a language of purely physical (and chemical, biological, and neurological) vocabulary L_{phys}. We want to extend this language to a language $L_{phys+psy}$ that includes the vocabulary of psychology, with predicates that assign beliefs, desires, and sensory experiences to a class of sentient and rational bodies (the human beings). Lewis assumes that we are already given, not only the vocabulary of $L_{phys+psy}$, but also a fairly rich theory of folk psychology T_{folk}, that specifies a large number of connections between psychological and physical states. This will include facts about the sensory experiences resulting from sensory-organ stimulations, coordinated in such a way that experiences are veridical under normal conditions. It will also include connections between belief-desire pairs and overt behavior, and certain kinds of overt behavior that results directly from certain experiences or desires, like wincing from pain.

- Let's assume that T_{folk} is consistent with the set of physical truths, $TRUE_{phys}$.
- If so, we can find an interpretation function $I_{phys+psy}$, relative to which T_{folk} is true in the true model of the physical world, $M_{true-phys}$.
- If there is such a function, it will be a realization (in Ramsey's sense) of the folk theory of psychology.

- If there is a unique such function, then we can use it to define the set of all psychological and psychophysical truths by simply identifying it with the set of sentences $\text{TRUE}_{phys+psy}$ in the language $L_{phys+psy}$ that are verified by the model $M_{true\text{-}phys}$ as extended by the interpretation function $I_{phys+psy}$.

Lewis is entitled to help himself to the psychophysical language $L_{phys+psy}$ and the folk theory T_{folk} in that theory, since the facts about what language humans speak and what sentences in that language they assert can be recovered with a high degree of determinacy from the physicalistically and behavioristically acceptable set of facts, simply by consulting users' overt verbal behavior (including their counterfactual behavior under all possible circumstances). This is the sort of task that Donald Davidson described as radical interpretation. (Davidson 1973) In any case, overt linguistic behavior (as described in TRUE_{phys}) would place very severe constraints on acceptable candidates for the language $L_{phys+psy}$ and the folk theory T_{folk}.

In addition to or as an alternative to reliance on the folk theory T_{folk}, we could rely, as Donald Davidson recommended, on a Principle of Charity, which could serve as a constraint on acceptable interpretation functions. We could require that the interpretation of sentences that attribute the belief with content ϕ be assigned intensions in which ϕ is also verified, at least to as great an extent as possible. We could also apply a similar Principle of Charity to the assignment of sensory and mnemonic contents to human subjects, along with a Principle of Humanity or Reasonableness that requires that beliefs be reasonable, given a subject's sensory and mnemonic information.

5.4 Wallace's Everettian Functionalism

In a sense, Wallace's functionalism, inspired by Daniel Dennett's Real Patterns (Dennett 1991), is a combination of phenomenalism and analytical functionalism, with mental properties reduced to macroscopic (and

chemical and biological) properties in something in the form of Lewis's Analytical Functionalism, and macroscopic properties further
reduced to states of the quantum wavefunction, in something like Russell's Structuralism.
The difficulty with this strategy, as we'll see,
is that this leaves us trying to lift ourselves by
our own bootstraps, with too little basis for
constraining the kinds of emergent domains
that can emerge.

It's reasonably clear what the reducing or
fundamental model is supposed to be. We can
take the language of pure quantum mechanics
(with its description of the cosmic wavefunction and its deterministic Schrödinger evolution) and supplement it with a counterfactual
or subjunctive conditional. This will require a
model that contains a domain of worlds, each
of which consists of a single quantum wavefunction evolved through time, one world designated as actual (which picks out the world's
actual wavefunction), and a system of spheres
S for the evaluation of subjunctive conditionals (the worlds of these models will not be
Everettian branches, but different versions of
the underlying quantum wavefunction). The

system of spheres could be based, as in David Lewis's semantics for subjunctive conditionals (Lewis 1973), on a relation of comparative similarity between quantum worlds. This would require something beyond pure quantum theory, and in that sense Wallacian functionalism does, like other interpretations of quantum mechanics, require some substantial supplementation to the theory.

In Wallace's proposal, the only constraint on the Ramsey realization of the emergent theory is this: all fillers of functional roles in the emergent theories must be entities and sets of entities to be found in the correct model of the formal language of pure quantum mechanics. In particular, there are no constraints on the extended interpretation function that can be expressed in terms of causal connections between emergent and quantum-mechanical entities or pure semantic conditions (such as metaphysically correct reference or truth-conditions for the emergent language) or metaphysical priority (no degrees of naturalness or eligibility that apply to sets of n-tuples quantum-mechanical entities), as I will argue in Section 5.6 below.

So, let's turn now to the emergent domain. Our first problem is a very basic one: What language do we use, and what theory in that language? In the case of phenomenalism, we had the common vocabulary of geometry and the necessary laws of perspective to constrain the language and theory of the emergent domain of physical objects. In the case of Analytical Functionalism, we had a folk theory of psychology and psychophysics that could be recovered from, or at least powerfully constrained by, the overt verbal behavior of human beings, all of which was contained within the base model of fundamental things. In addition, the beliefs and sensory states attributed by the emergent theory have contents that match the vocabulary of the base theory. Now, we have only the language and theory of pure quantum mechanics to begin with, which by itself tells us nothing about the languages and beliefs of the denizens of an emergent world, and which lacks the direct access to our beliefs and concepts of the physical environment, as was available for the phenomenalist.

So, it seems that we must use every possible language and every possible theory. There are no languages or theories and no language users or believers explicit at the level of quantum reality. Any constraints we place on these theories (besides their sheer interpretability in the model of quantum mechanics) are going to be constraints of internal coherency. That is, we might reasonably demand of any theory $T_{emergent}$ of the emergent world that, according to $T_{emergent}$ itself, the human beings speak the language of $T_{emergent}$ and have beliefs and sensory and mnemonic experiences that mostly accord with $T_{emergent}$. We can also require that $T_{emergent}$ have the theoretical virtues valued by most people (as depicted in $T_{emergent}$), and that $T_{emergent}$ be well-confirmed, according to itself. Call the theories that meet these constraints the internally ideal or coherent theories.

5.5 Putnam's Permutation Argument for Semantic Indeterminacy

I will argue, in a way inspired by Putnam's argument for metaphysical anti-realism (Putnam 1978, 1980, 1981, Lewis 1984), that there is a radical indeterminacy of meaning and intension for all the names, predicates, and function symbols of the languages of our emergent theories. This isn't surprising, since all of the entities and properties posited by such theories are, from the point of view of Wallacian functionalism, mere useful fictions. In Wallace's picture, all that matters is that we find an interpretation of those theories in the true model of quantum mechanics that makes all of the formulas of that theory come out true (or at least approximately true) under that interpretation. The meaning of the emergent theories, the theories of the world's manifest image, is utterly holistic in character.

Suppose that $T_{emergent}$ is a theory of a world that is emergent relative to the model $M_{true\text{-}QM}$. That means that there is an interpretation function, call it $I_{intended}$ that extends I to the language of $T_{emergent}$, resulting in a new model $M_{QM+emergent}$.with the theory $T_{emergent}$ true in $M_{QM+emergent}$. It is immediately obvious that there are an infinite number of alternative extensions of I that will also produce an extension of $M_{true\text{-}QM}$ relative to which $T_{emergent}$ is true. Take any permutation $\pi(w)$ for any world $w \in W$ of the objects that exist in w (according to the model). Now apply the permutation $\pi(w)$ to the interpretation $I_{intended}$ with respect to the interpretation of all constants and predicate symbols at w. The resulting interpretation $I_{intended\text{-}\pi(w)}$ will also be a realization of $T_{emergent}$. Apply similar permutations to every world in W, resulting in the thoroughly scrambled interpretation $I_{bizarro}$. The extension of $M_{true\text{-}QM}$ by $I_{bizarro}$ will also be a model of $T_{emergent}$, and so $I_{bizarro}$ will be a realization of $T_{emergent}$ in $M_{true\text{-}QM}$.

So, for example, it is completely indeterminate what a predicate like 'is human' or 'is conscious' is true of or realized by. In the interpretation function $I_{bizarro}$, the intention of human beings might be the intention of kumquats in $I_{intended}$, and the interpretation of 'is conscious' might be 'contains vitamin B.' In fact, as Alexander Pruss (Pruss 2015b) has pointed out, all the predicates that apply truthfully to the emergent world as it exists today (including mental-property predicates) could be interpreted in such a way that they apply truthfully only to the cosmos as it was 12 billion years ago.

Here is the key difference between Wallacian functionalism and the phenomenalistic functionalism of a Mill or Carnap, or the behavioristic functionalism of David Lewis. In the case of a phenomenalistic functionalism, the fundamental or base theory is a theory of our phenomenological experience, and the target or reduced theory is one of the "external" world. In this case, there is arguably some constraint on the content of the reduced theory that is non-holistic. For example, in the case of the primary qualities, we could insist that the geometrical properties assigned to physical objects in our external theory resemble the geometrical properties of the corresponding inner phenomena. So, if the external theory asserts the existence of something tetrahedral in shape, we could insist that the corresponding model of the phenomenal world include something that at least appears tetrahedral (perhaps, a two-dimensional projection in visual space of a tetrahedron). However, in the case of Wallacian functionalism, there are no phenomenal qualia on either side of the equation. There are only sentences in our folk psychology assigning certain geometrical experiences to subjects, and so long as the interpretation of these sentences preserves their truth and their counterfactual inter-connections, we have met every constraint on a successful interpretation.

In the case of behavioristic functionalism, we have real connections between the subjects of psychological states on the one hand and the subjects of behavior on the other. We assign beliefs and desires to x in a way that corresponds rationally to the behavior of x. In the case of Wallacian functionalism, we have only the universal wave function on the side of the base theory. All real or fundamental behavior is ultimately behavior of that function, and so there are no localized constraints on the connections between belief and desire and behavior. It is the theory of the folkish world as a whole (with both human belief and behavior contained in a single package) that confronts the model of pure QM as a whole.

In addition, Wallacian functionalists lack any of the resources used by metaphysical realists to meet the challenge of Putnam's argument: causal ties between emergent terms and their quantum-mechanical referents, especially eligible or natural properties (at a phenomenological level), so-called "reference magnets," or metaphysically primitive facts about semantics or reference. (For more details, see Koons 2018b.)

There is one particular case of referential indeterminacy that is especially devastating to the Everettian interpretation: namely, it is indeterminate whether a particular emergent world is assigned to quantum states with a high or low amplitude. Thus, there is no objective fact of the matter about whether the quantum probability associated with a given "branch" is high or low. Thus, the problem is not just that of finding a reason for believing that we are in a high amplitude branch. The problem is that we cannot give any real meaning to the question itself. If a given emergent world is realizable in a low-probability segment of the wavefunction at a given time, there is another interpretation function (and thus another realization of that world in that wavefunction) that assigns it to a high-probability segment, and vice versa. It is all a matter of performing the appropriate permutation of quantum objects.

If there is no objective matter of fact about the quantum probabilities corresponding to the various emergent realities, then the Deutsch-Saunders-Wallace strategy for defending the reliability of observed statistics is further undermined. Emergent realities in which the statistics radically disconfirm quantum mechanics will be, not only as real as our own, but possessing the same status in regard to the underlying quantum probabilities. They will have just as much right to claim to be realized in the high-amplitude sectors of the quantum wavefunction as do the QM-confirming branches.

5.6 Indeterminacy Guarantees Truth of All Emergent Theories

Let $T_{emergent}$ be one of our target theories of the world: folk psychology or a scientific theory of "emergent" phenomena. We can suppose that $T_{emergent}$ is internally ideal and that it has a realization in the model of quantum mechanics, $M_{\text{true-QM}}$. Let I_{intended} be the "intended" interpretation of the theory T_{emergent} in the model $M_{\text{true-QM}}$, with a domain consisting of the spacetime regions and quantum subsystems of the quantum world and with the predicates of the language L_{emergent} assigned appropriate intensions in the corresponding model $M_{\text{true-QM}}$.

Now consider a theory T_{bizarro}, whose intended model includes the same interpretation function I_{intended} but includes a different, counterfactual model of the quantum world, $M_{\text{counterfactual-QM}}$. Both $M_{\text{true-QM}}$ and $M_{\text{counterfactual-QM}}$ have infinite models, and both T_{emerge} and T_{bizarro} are semantically consistent with the hypothesis of a domain of infinite cardinality. By the Skolem-Löwenheim theorems, there is an interpretation I_{bizarro} of T_{bizarro} in the actual model of the quantum world, $M_{\text{true-QM}}$. Thus, the bizarro emergent world represented by T_{bizarro} is realized in the actual quantum world in just the same way as T_{emergent} is.

In fact, all possible theories of emergent domains are actually true: if they are logically consistent (in the logic of quantified counterfactual conditionals), and they contain no quantum-mechanical vocabulary and make no claims about the finite size of reality, then (by the Skolem-Löwenheim theorems), they have a model that extends $M_{\text{true-QM}}$. In fact, just this point was made by H. A. Newman in 1928 (Newman 1928), as a criticism of Russell's structuralism.

In fact, the situation is even worse than this, since Wallace doesn't require perfect realization in $M_{\text{true-QM}}$—just a reasonable degree of approximation to such perfect realization. So, even inconsistent theories or theories that entail the existence of a finite domain or that entail falsehoods about the structure of spacetime will nonetheless have quantum realizations and so will be actually true theories of a world that emerges from the quantum world.

The upshot is this: we are free to believe and say whatever we want about the emergent world of macroscopic objects, and we are guaranteed to believe and speak the truth (so long as our stories are internally coherent and not massively inconsistent). As a result, every consistent story corresponds to a real, emergent world, on par with our own. This includes the world of Tolkien's mythology or that of H. P. Lovecraft, the world of Harry Potter or Greek mythology. They are all just as real as our own. And, even more importantly, our own theory of the emergent world is true by a kind of stipulation: true simply by virtue of satisfying our demands for its internal coherency.

But that surely is wrong. If our theory of the emergent world is true by a kind of stipulation, then it can't be interpreted realistically. To interpret it realistically is to take seriously the metaphysical possibility that it could be wrong. For example, all of the evidence we have for classical mechanics could be misleading ("could" metaphysically, not "epistemically"): it could have been produced by some other quite unknown mechanism. For example, the planetary orbits that led to Kepler's laws and ultimately to Newton's laws of motion could actually have resulted from the fact that the planets move on gigantic rails built by ancient aliens. For the theory of classical mechanics to be a substantive theory of the world, it must have the metaphysical possibility of being wrong. But Wallace's functionalism denies it that chance.

5.7 Epistemological and Pragmatic Consequences

If classical physics is understood as true by stipulation, this undermines any rational confidence we might have in quantum mechanics, since a large part of our evidence for QM consists in its agreement with classical mechanics when interference terms are small.

In fact, Wallace's functionalism leads quickly to an epistemological catastrophe: if we cannot interpret our theories of the emergent world realistically, then no belief in such a theory can count as objective knowledge. And yet all of our knowledge of the truth of quantum mechanics depends on our having objective knowledge of experimental data that belongs to an emergent domain. So, in the end, Wallacian functionalism is epistemologically self-defeating, destroying the only grounds we have for believing that quantum mechanics is true at all, to say nothing of believing that it exhausts the fundamental level of reality.

In fact, we couldn't even interpret our emergent scientific theories as instrumentally valuable in an objective way, since any theory of our future experiences would be equally true (just one more realizable emergent theory). In addition, what counts as the same qualitative properties of experience is itself up for grabs via the interpretation function. By choosing a suitable function, we can make any set of predictions about future experience come out true.

Thus, pragmatism itself is inconsistent with radical indeterminacy of meaning, as Plato recognized in the Theaetetus:

> SOCRATES But, Protagoras (we'll say), what about the things which are going to be, in the future? Does he [the individual human being] have in himself the authority for deciding about them, too? If someone thinks there's going to be a thing of some kind, does that thing actually come into being for the

person who thought so? Take heat, for example. Suppose a layman thinks he's going to catch a fever and there's going to be that degree of heat, whereas someone else, a doctor, thinks not. Which one's judgment shall we say the future will turn out to accord with? Or should we say that it will be in accordance with the judgments of both: for the doctor he'll come to be neither hot nor feverish, whereas for himself he'll come to be both?

THEODORUS. No, that would be absurd. [Plato 2014, p. 56, 178c1–10]

Every claim about the future, practical consequences about believing and acting on an emergent theory of the world will itself be part of some emergent theory of the world. I have shown that every such theory, so long as it is not massively inconsistent and doesn't entail the finitude of the universe, will be realizable in $M_{\text{true-QM}}$ and so will be true. Thus, we cannot appeal to pragmatic considerations (like avoiding being eaten by a tiger) as grounds for preferring some theories over others.

5.8 The Argument in a Nutshell

To sum up, there are four disastrous consequences for Wallacian functionalism:

- Radical indeterminacy of content, via Putnam's paradox: there an infinite number of alternative interpretation functions mapping our actual theory of the world into M_{QM}. In particular, there is no fact of the matter as to the quantum probability associated with any given emergent world.
- Every consistent and internally coherent story (more precisely, every story consistent with an infinite domain) represents an emergent reality in M_{QM}, on a par with our current best theories about the macroscopic world.
- So, we can't go wrong in proposing theories about the emergent world we inhabit,

so long as our theories are consistent with an infinite domain, and so long as they are internally coherent from a semantic and epistemological point of view.

- These facts undermine any claim to know that quantum mechanics is true, on the basis of experiments and observations that depend in any way on the emergent. The impossibility of objectively false theories of the emergent domain makes objective knowledge of that domain impossible, including objective knowledge of the data and observations upon which we ground our claims to know the truth of quantum mechanics itself. Therefore, Wallacian functionalism is epistemologically self-defeating.

5.9 The Solution: Real Essences and Traveling Forms

My real complaint is with Daniel Dennett's "Real Patterns" (Dennett 1991), which is the original inspiration for Wallace's functionalism. I believe, in fact, that my arguments in section 5.6 above would apply with almost equal force to any functionalist account of the emergent world, including Bohmian interpretations of quantum mechanics.

The problem for Dennett is this: What makes a pattern *real*? As we have seen, mere realizability in the true quantum model of the world does not suffice. Here is the crux of the problem: we have to construct both the theory and its semantics simultaneously, with an aim toward maximizing simplicity (in both dimensions). What then keeps us from simply collapsing into the identity isomorphism and the trivial theory? If we had a fixed theory and had to find the simplest semantics, or if we had a fixed semantics and had to find the simplest theory, the problem would be well defined and constrained.

We need some top-down constraint. It also has to be an ontological constraint: a set of natural kinds of emergent entities, each with a fixed real essence. These essences can then constrain both the story and the story's semantics. But to carry this out, we can't be physicalists—we can't limit the fundamental structure of reality to what can be described exclusively in quantum-mechanical terms. When things have real essences, they must be real.

What's needed is a coherent account of a macroscopic world that co-exists with QM. And the very existence of such a world falsifies the claim that the quantum-mechanical exhausts the fundamental structure of reality. The real essences of macroscopic entities must be co-fundamental with the quantum-mechanical facts.

Once we posit new entities with their own essences that can explain (in a top-down fashion) those entities' grounding in the quantum domain, we open up the possibility that these composite, macroscopic entities (and not just their essences) are also ontologically fundamental: metaphysically dependent on but not wholly grounded in (not fully explainable in terms of) the micro-quantum realm. In particular, there could be a diachronic and causal component to the answer to van Inwagen's Special Composition Question (van Inwagen 1990, pp. 21–22): the existence of a composite macro-object on a certain branch of the cosmic wavefunction might be causally dependent on the prior existence of composite objects in that branch in the immediately preceding period, that is, partly dependent on composite objects in that branch with the required fundamental causal powers. This would of course fit well with Aristotle's vision of the world, in which the generation of new composite substances is always the result of the "corruption" of pre-existing substances, with the processes of corruption and generation being explainable in terms of the exercise of active and passive causal powers by participants in the processes. On a hylomorphic interpretation of Everettian quantum mechanics, the state of the quantum wavefunction (in particular, the presence of decoherent branches) is the material cause of the existence of certain composite, macroscopic entities. But the quantum function by itself is not a metaphysically sufficient ground or explanation: in addition, there must be a formal cause, reflecting the real essence of a natural kind of macroscopic, composite object. The presence of such a substantial form in a branch of the cosmic wavefunction at a particular place and time would have a diachronic causal explanation, which could make reference to earlier facts at the emergent scale in the branch in the spatial neighborhood of the persisting or newly generated composite substance.

The natural kinds will make a real difference by virtue of constraining acceptable models to connect substances of each kind with appropriate branches in the branching-extension of M_{QM}.

Bonus: Restoring the Real World's Unity

Once we have real essences at the macroscopic level, we have the real possibility of diachronic, horizontal causation at that same level. In particular, we can consider positing a dynamic element to the solution of van Inwagen's Special Composition Question. We can call the result the traveling forms interpretation of quantum mechanics. This interpretation has some similarity to Jeffrey Barrett's single-mind interpretation (Barrett 1995), except where Barrett has a cohort of conscious minds traveling through the branching structure of the Many Worlds version, the traveling forms interpretation has instead a cohort of composite macroscopic objects. In Barrett's interpretation, all branches but one are occupied by zombies, by living human bodies that lack consciousness. In Barrett's picture, it is the presence of real consciousness that picks out the uniquely actual branch.

On my traveling forms interpretation, in contrast, all branches but one are occupied by pluralities of particles that fail to compose anything at all. We might call these pluralities of fundamental quantum particles "compositional zombies." Although they have, from the microphysical perspective, everything that is needed for the potential existence of macroscopic objects (stars, planets, organisms, macro-molecules), no actual composite entities correspond to these branches. They are occupied wholly by compositional zombies.

Thus, the traveling forms version is not committed to anything like substance dualism: it is consistent with the supervenience of the mental on the physical, so long as the physical includes facts about which particles compose larger physical wholes. It does, however, deny that the compositional facts about physical entities supervene on the microphysical or quantum facts alone. Whether a branch corresponds to a domain of actual composite physical objects will depend on two factors: (1) Does the branch satisfy decoherence to a sufficient degree of exactitude (a degree determined by the real essences of composite physical kinds)? And, (2) Has the branch been occupied by composite objects in the immediate past, composite objects that are disposed either to persist in time or to generate new composite objects? In addition, there is a third, indeterministic factor: whenever a branch splits into two potential macroworlds, the substantial forms responsible for composition jointly actualize macroscopic composition in just one of the new branches, with a probability normally determined by Born's rule (i.e., a probability proportional to the square of the amplitude of each branch).

I talk of *traveling* forms because I want to relate this interpretation to the Aristotelian theory of substantial forms. A substantial form is something (a principle or process) that is responsible for making what would otherwise be a mere cloud or heap of smaller entities into a single composite substance. For Aristotelians, a substance is an entity that is primary in the order of existence, an entity that has unity to the highest degree (per se unity) and which is the bearer of fundamental causal powers. It is an axiom of Aristotelian metaphysics that no substance is composed of other substances. Substances stand at the top of the compositional hierarchy. For more details, see the chapter by Alexander Pruss (Pruss 2018).

5.10 Conclusion

Clearly, what's needed to rescue Wallace's picture is some further constraint on the interpretation function. Wallace's intention is surely that this extra constraint should have something to do with decoherence, with a linkage of some kind between macroscopic and quantum dynamics. However, as we have seen, the functionalist model that Wallace adopts, following the lead of Dennett's "Real Patterns" (Dennett 1991), won't deliver what is needed.

Ultimately, the extra constraint must have

a top-down salient to it: it must derive somehow from the real essences of macroscopic substances (in Aristotle's sense, primary beings). But once we add these new element of constraint, it will be hard to resist the temptation to move still farther away from the Everettian picture. The essences of macroscopic substances can give rise to novel causal powers at that level, causal powers that can determine which branch of the quantum wavefunction is really occupied by composite substances of the appropriate kind, restoring a single, unified world to the picture and thereby avoiding the twin problems of possible trans-world values and of anti-Darwinian branches.

Chapter 6

Biology and Human Sciences after the Counter-Revolution

6.1 Quantum Statistical Mechanics and Chemistry

The Aristotelian interpretation of quantum statistical mechanics and quantum chemistry can be summarized in three points.

1. The presence of the substantial form (unifying essence) of a thermal substance grounds the fact that the substance constitutes a thermodynamic system with infinitely many virtual parts, each

corresponding to a finite sub-region of a continuum of matter (represented by the "continuum limit").

2. The virtual presence of infinitely many sub-systems grounds the fundamental properties of thermodynamics (heat, temperature), classical superselection sectors (phase transitions and other broken symmetries), and temporal irreversibility.

3. These thermal properties ground (in a top-down fashion) enduring chemical structures, with molecules (including chiral molecules) as either virtual or integral parts of the thermal substance (depending on context and history).

Spontaneous symmetry-breaking, including spatially asymmetrical molecular structures, arise naturally in the setting of infinite quantum-mechanical models. We can therefore explain why large molecules and other molecules in dynamic interaction with their environment have stable molecular structures, despite the prevalence of superpositions at the quantum level.

The world is composed entirely of living organisms and extra-organismic thermal substances. Everything else is either a virtual or integral part of such a substance, or a remnant of a substance, or a heap or aggregate of such entities. Generalized quantum mechanics gives us good grounds for believing in the existence of exactly the sort of thermal substances needed to satisfy the Tiling Constraint. The chemical and thermodynamic properties of the thermal substances constitute their form; the quantum potentialities of their virtual parts, their matter. The virtual, quantum parts of substances lack definite location (contrary to Aristotle's expectation), enabling the possibility of long-range entanglement at that level.

As we have seen in Chapter 3, molecular structure is a relational rather than an intrinsic property of molecules. So are thermodynamic properties like temperature. A robust version of hylomorphic escalation would hold the biological domain responsible to a significant degree for the macroscopic structuring of the chemical and microphysical domains. Think of the role of stitching that holds together the patches in a patchwork quilt: thermodynamics and chemistry are responsible for the internal structure of the patches (the atoms and molecules), biology for their determinate spatial and dynamical inter-relationships. This doesn't require any new fundamental forces—no *vis vitalis*.

Even a robust conception of free will can find a natural home in this framework: free will is just one more kind of spontaneous symmetry-breaking, of much the same sort as we saw in the context of thermodynamics, with the difference that the symmetry that's broken is psycho-physiological rather than chemical. Spontaneous symmetry-breaking means that we human beings can be in a state that is, insofar as it is grounded entirely at the micro-level, a symmetrical superposition of both possible choices, but which at the social and human level must take one definite form or the other, in a way that is not fixed from the bottom up. This does have the consequence that the human level could be indeterministic even if the quantum level is (taken on its own) deterministic.

6.2 Irreducible Powers of Organisms

How do organisms fit into the world of thermal substances? Thermal substances have a *virtual* presence within an organism. These virtually present thermal substances correspond to actual quantitative parts of the organism, contributing to the explanation of the causal powers of those parts. Consequently, there is a metaphysically fundamental difference between inorganic water (for example) and water as it exists in organisms, although clearly inorganic water can play a role of material causation or explanation in relation to organic processes, even if organic and inorganic water are empirically indistinguishable in their chemical actions. The chemical properties of the water have different metaphysical explanations, depending on the kind of substance (thermal or organic) to which it belongs.

The chemical and thermodynamic properties and the associated causal powers that the quantitative parts of the living body possess are partly determined by the *soul*, the substantial form of the body, along with the *holistic* accidents of the organism, like perception or thought. The interaction is not one of action/passion, as between two substances, but top-down formal determination. Nonetheless, changeable mental attributes can make a real difference to the operation of bodily parts, and vice versa. The soul can guide the breaking of microscopic symmetries, imposing asymmetric accidents on the results, without requiring any novel force (such as Bergson's *élan vital*) or violation of conservation laws.

Is there immanent teleology in nature outside of human thought and intention? Thomists and other Aristotelians argue that the answer is Yes. In fact, whenever a thing acts according to its intrinsic power and potentialities, immanent teleology exists (Rota 2011). Fundamental causal powers as Aristotle conceives of them are *inherently teleological*. To have the power to produce E in circumstances C is to have the C-to-E transition as one of one's natural functions. Indeed, as George Molnar (2003) has pointed out, the ontology of causal powers builds *intentional-ity* into the very foundations of natural things. To have a power is to be in a kind of intentional state, one that is in a real sense "about" the effects one is predisposed to produce.

In the Aristotelian model, biological teleology requires just two things: a robust causal powers metaphysics, and *real causal powers* at the level of biological organs and organisms. Such real powers require, in turn, substantial forms at the level of whole organisms. The substantial form of an organism is called its soul (*psyche*). In non-human animals and in plants, the soul is non-rational. Human souls possess additional rational powers, powers of scientific understanding and deliberation about the good.

This emergence of new powers at the macroscopic, biological scale should be unsurprising, given the fact that, according to our most recent quantum mechanical models, we see strong (ontological) emergence at the mesoscopic scale in solid-state physics and chemistry. Mesoscopic systems, like ferromagnets, superconductors, and Bose-Einstein condensates, all exhibit dynamical behaviors that are irreducible to the microstates of the constituent particles, namely spontaneous symmetry-breaking and thermodynamic irreversibility. In a similar way, we should expect the biological functioning of organisms to be irreducible to the chemical and thermodynamic facts about the virtual thermal substances that correspond to their actual quantitative parts.

Evolution itself presupposes teleology in the very idea of *reproduction*, and so evolution requires irreducible causal powers at the organismic level. No organism ever produces an exact physical duplicate of itself. In the case of sexual reproduction, the children are often not even close physical approximations to either parent at any stage. An organism successfully *reproduces* itself when it successfully produces another instance of its own *biological kind*. This presupposes a form of teleological realism, since biological kinds are individuated teleologically, that is, in terms of their fundamental causal powers.

Richard Dawkins has suggested that we think of organisms as mere "robots" that our DNA molecules have "programmed" for reproducing themselves (Dawkins 1976, xxi). In fact, DNA molecules never succeed in producing perfect physical duplicates of themselves, and even if they did, the mere physical duplication of the molecule would not constitute reproducing oneself. Suppose, for example, that an eccentric billionaire builds a chemical factory that does nothing but fill barrels with copies of his own genome, launching them into deep space. No one would think that such a man had succeeded in procreating trillions of descendants. A DNA molecule counts as a copy of one of one's genes only when it is successfully fulfilling the function of a gene within a living organism, indeed, within a living organism of the appropriate teleologically-defined kind.

6.3 Biological Normativity

Alexander Pruss and I have argued that functionalist theories of mind require an account of *normativity* (Koons and Pruss 2017, Simpson forthcoming). The argument can be extended to functionalist accounts of biology. The functional dispositions that are supposed to be definitive of mental or biological states can only be defined relative to the *normal* state of the organism, where the "normality" involved is a normative notion, *not* merely a matter of averages or actual frequencies. There are two prima facie plausible accounts of the natural basis of normativity: Aristotelian powers and evolutionary accounts.

An Aristotelian can give a straightforward account of such normativity:

> A substance is *supposed to* produce E on occasions of C if and only if its nature includes a C-to-E power.

The other potential source of normativity is evolutionary selection. For example, Ruth Millikan (1984) attempted define normality in terms of adaptations:

> If a system x belongs to a reproductive family F, then x is supposed to produce E under circumstances C if and only if doing so is one of F's *adaptations*.

This seems to be the most promising alternative to the Aristotelian account. However, such evolutionary accounts are highly vulnerable to hypothetical counter-examples. Pruss proposed (in Koons and Pruss 2017) the thought-experiment of the Great Grazing Ground: a hypothetical world in which organisms in our history were maximally proficient in reproduction, thanks to the intervention of benevolent aliens. In such a world, even if the causal path leading to each of us were identical to the actual historical path, none of us would be conscious, since no distinction between normal and abnormal states could exist. Without that distinction, the relevant functional states supposedly defining consciousness could not be instantiated.

Pruss's thought experiment brings out very vividly how Millikan's definition of biological teleology fails to capture any form of immanent teleology. The present function of an organ or organelle depends on her definition on remote facts in the past, and even on past facts that are causally unrelated to the present. If human thought and intention depend on the teleology of the human body, then thought and intention are also extrinsic to our present constitution and operation, which is incredible.

6.4 Secondary Qualities

An Aristotelian account of organisms provides clear advantages for epistemology. Take, for example, our perception of secondary qualities. Unless we are perceiving real qualities in nature, and qualities that really are as we perceive them to be, all of our empirical knowledge is vulnerable to skeptical challenge. Microphysicalists cannot suppose that secondary qualities (as we perceive them) are real, since scientific theory has no place for any counterpart to color, smell, etc. at the microphysical level. In contrast, hylomorphists can suppose thermal substances to have fundamental powers of mutual interaction that correspond closely with the appearance of color, sound, and odor. The quantum-level interactions of particles are less, rather than more, fundamental than these chromatic, acoustic, and olfactory interactions between thermal substances. Organisms have evolved fundamental passive powers of responding reliably to these active powers, resulting in veridical perception of the qualitative features of inorganic substances. This provides a metaphysical foundation for J. J. Gibson's (1979) ecological theory of color, rehabilitating the "secondary" qualities to first-class status.

Anti-realists about secondary qualities could object that the hylomorphic view fails to secure the veridicality of color perception, since colors *as they appear to us* are categorical (non-dispositional) and non-relational, while the qualities of thermal substances are merely powers to affect other substances. But in a causal-powers ontology, the activation of a causal power *is* a categorical and intrinsic property of its bearer. When we perceive the color of a substance, we are perceiving an accident of *action*, the actualization of a corresponding power to act. An accident of action can both be intrinsic to a substance and make essential reference to something beyond it. The critic is right in thinking that colors as we perceive them are not perceived as the actualization of something relative to *us*, but as the actualization of a mind-independent feature. That aspect of our phenomenology is preserved in the Aristotelian account, since the qualities involve powers to act on *both* inorganic thermal substances and our sensory organs.

6.5 Evolution

But is the Aristotelian account of organisms compatible with the facts of biological evolution? Wasn't Aristotle committed to the eternal fixity of the species? In fact, the fixity of species is no more central to Aristotle's system than is the constancy of the celestial spheres. Aristotle's natural philosophy depends on the existence of individual substantial forms, and to the existence of relations of objective resemblance between those forms, resulting in a nested, species-genus structure of taxonomy. All of these features are fully compatible with (and even partly explained by) the theory of evolution. And, as I argued earlier in this section, evolution actually *depends on* the existence of organismic substantial forms.

In principle, there would be no problem for hylomorphism even if every biological individual were ontologically *sui generis*. And the transition from one species to another is not a problem. Aristotle recognized that the environment plays a role, along with the parents, in every case of reproduction: "man and the sun beget man" (*Physics* ii.2, 194b13).

But Aristotle's theory does require a principled distinction between substantial forms and mere accidents, and a neo-Darwinian theory would seem to blur that distinction, supposing that the essence of a biological individual consists of nothing but the accumulation of favored accidents. Darwinian evolution depends on a pre-existing genetic variety within species, which corresponds (in Aristotelian terms) to the members' possession of contrary contingent accidents. As a new species emerges, what had been mere contingent accidents take on new functions, enabling the organisms with those accidents to better exploit some ecological niche. Therefore, it seems, at least *prima facie*, that all evolutionary change involves merely changes in the distribution of accidents within related populations. Where is the need for the substantial form and its essence?

For Aristotelians, the distinction between substantial form and accident depends on a set of asymmetric explanatory relations. A substantial form explains the organism's potentiality for certain accidents, and not vice versa. This is compatible with neo-Darwinian theory, which is silent on the explanatory priority between biological forms.

For hylomorphists, there is a traditional distinction between "proper" and contingent accidents. An accident is proper (a *proprium*) if it flows from the specific nature of the substantial form; otherwise, it is contingent.[24] Among contingent accidents, some are permanent (like sex or handedness) and others are changeable. The permanent but contingent accidents are explained by the combination of the nature of the substantial form with certain contingent facts about the process by which the organism was generated and originally developed. Changeable accidents are explained by combining the nature of the substantial form with contingent facts about the subsequent history of the organism.

Now, the crucial question is: can the Aristotelian explain how some accident could be

24 Although propria are fully explained by a substance's essence, it is possible for a substance to lack one of its propria, through genetic defect or injury. Being bipedal is a proprium of human nature, but not all human beings have two legs in fact.

a contingent accident of an ancestral form of the organism but a proper accident of the organism itself (or vice versa)? Doesn't this require a sharp, un-Darwinian transition between one generation (for which the accident is contingent) and the next one (for which the accident is proper)?

Not necessarily. It could be that during evolution a population comes to realize (unstably) substantial forms that belong simultaneously to two distinct species. The substances in such a population would have two, contrary propria, each one a differentia of a different species. Each member of the population would be abnormal relative to one or both of its species, lacking one or both of the contrary propria. Relative to one species, the accident is permanent but contingent, and relative to the other it is proper. In such a population, there would be an unusual and unstable over-determination in the explanation of the possession of certain proper accidents. The presence of a proper accident that is a differentia of one of the two species would be explained twice over: once by direct implication from one of the specific natures of the substantial form, and in another way by contingent factors in the substance's generation and development that result in the organism's deformation relative to the other species. The transitional organism's substantial form would have a natural disposition toward both contrary differentiae. This would be an unusual situation, but not an impossible one.

Alternatively, even if it were true that each organism must belong to a unique species, this would not create an insuperable problem for reconciling Aristotle and evolution. We could suppose that transitional populations consist of a mixture of two species, with members of each species able to mate with the other, and with offspring of both species possible from a single pair of parents.[25]

25 It is important to note that metaphysical species do not necessarily correspond 1-to-1 with what biologists mean by 'species'. Biologists use a number of criteria to distinguish one species from another, and none of these criteria will always carve nature at the joints, metaphysically speaking. Nonetheless, just as new species in the various biological senses arise by descent with modification, the same must be true of metaphysical species.

The co-existence of distinct species would reflect the fact that the population stands on a
borderline between two competing explanatory schemes. Some organisms will fall one
side of the boundary or the other, due to its
particular configuration of accidents.

Eventually, selective pressures could elim-
inate the representation in the population of
the older species, completing the origin of a
new species, which would eventually become
reproductively isolated. The Aristotelian concept of species would not perfectly coincide
with modern biological uses in evolutionary
settings, but the correspondence would in general be quite close.

6.6 Conclusion

Aristotelian pluralism carves a middle path
between atomism and cosmic monism, securing a foundation for the manifest image of
human life. It acknowledges the homeliness of
the world—a place in which human freedom,
agency, and knowledge can exist without
threat of nihilism or corrosive skepticism.
Modern science seemed to threaten this world

with a universal acid of atomistic reduction-ism, but the implications of the quantum rev-olution enable us to set the world right again.

The holistic and teleological character of quantum mechanics does not by itself vindi-cate the reality of teleology and agency at the biological or personal levels. However, it does dramatically change the imaginative land-scape of modern science, making the supposi-tion of top-down, formal causation in the realms of chemistry, thermodynamics, biol-ogy, and psychology plausible. In fact, the trend of science in the last fifty years has been toward greater differentiation, not unity. Tak-ing these scientific results at their face value means accepting causal agency (understood in Aristotelian terms) at many levels, including the macroscopic level of complete organisms. The idea that there could be a natural and fundamental teleology governing human choices is once again fully credible, and God as the ultimate source and ground of teleology is once again an attractive path for natural theology.

Chapter 7
Substances, Accidents, and Quantitative Parts

7.1 Accidents and Parts

The notion of a substance (Greek ousia, Latin *substantia*) is central to Aristotelianism. A substance is an entity with an essence or nature, in the strictest sense of the world. The essences of substances are metaphysically fundamental, in the sense that the essence of anything else is explained in part in terms of the essences of substances, while the essences of substances are explanatorily bedrock. The priority of substantial essence has a number of corollaries:

1. Substances are *fundamental* entities, in the sense that each substance has its own act or fact of actual existence, a fact that is not even partially grounded in the actual existence of anything else.[26]

2. Substances are *unified* in the strictest and most fundamental way. A substance is one thing, and its unity does not depend on anything distinct from it and its essence.[27]

---

26 More accurately, substances are composites of two fundamental entities (a substantial form and some prime matter), each of which is fundamental in a different way. The substantial form is a fundamental source of actual existence and of nature, while the prime matter contributes fundamental numerical distinctness from other substances of the same kind (Koons 2018d). Nonetheless, there is a sense in which it is substances that *exist* fundamentally, since the substantial form exists only in a secondary sense, by virtue of being the source of existence for the substance, and the prime matter derives its actual existence from the actual existence of the whole.

27 This also has to be qualified, since the substance is, in a sense, a *composite* of form and prime matter. However, neither the form nor the matter is a *part* of the substance in the ordinary

3. Substances *persist*, and the essences of substance do not change but are the grounds (at least partially) of all intrinsic change.

4. Substances are the fundamental bearers of *causal powers* (both active and passive) and so are the ultimate truthmakers of dynamic laws of nature.

Orthodox Aristotelians hold that the world contains more than one substance, and that it contains, in addition to substances, two further kinds of things (*res*): accidents and quantitative parts of substances. Therefore, Aristotelians accept two theses rejected by Democritean materialists (both ancient and modern): that there are composite substances, and that substances undergo intrinsic change. There are a variety of interpretations of

> sense of the word. The prime matter is simply the whole substance *qua* bare particular (*qua* unformed), and the substantial form exists by providing the substance with a fully unified existence, and substance is not itself one of the things that has to be unified with others in constituting the whole.

Aristotle (especially of *The Categories*) and a variety of contemporary versions of Aristotelianism that differ in their understanding of both accidents and parts. I will assume here (for the sake of simplicity) that accidents are abstract particulars and not universals (following Thomas Aquinas, and contrary to Michael Loux 2008 or David Armstrong 1996). I will also assume that quantitative parts of substances are neither accidents nor substances (in the strict sense), although they belong in a derivative way to the category of *substance*. The axiom that no substance can have other substances as parts is fundamental to the system, in my view. Aristotle, *Metaphysics* 1041a5 (Aristotle 1952): "No substance is composed of substances."

To use some helpful scholastic terminology, accidents can be either *proper* or *contingent*. A proper accident is one that flows necessarily from a substance's essence. It is an accident that the substance cannot be without, like the accident of humans of *being capable of laughter* (risibility). Nonetheless, there is a clear asymmetry between the substance's essence and any of its proper accidents: the essence explains why the substance has the proper accident, and not vice versa. So, for instance, human rationality explains risibility and not vice versa. Contingent accidents are crucial to the Aristotelian account of intrinsic change. When a substance undergoes intrinsic (non-Cambridge) change, it gains or loses some contingent accident.

We can distinguish between an accidental form, the accident itself, and the accidental unity that results from the accident's being-in the substance. So, for example, we can distinguish the form of Socrates' musicality (that *by which* he is musical), his musicality itself, and the accidental unity that is *musical Socrates*. The accidental form grounds the accident, and the accident is a component of the accidental unity. In the parlance of modern analytic philosophy, it is the accident that is a *property* or character of Socrates, while the form is the ground of that character, and the accidental unity is the whole Socrates as-qualified-by the accident. I have argued elsewhere that we should take seriously the existence of forms as distinct from properties, so I won't rehearse those arguments here (Koons 2018d). I also won't address whether accidental unities should be thought of as real or merely logical/notional beings. (One option is to think of them as wholes composed of substances and accidental forms—see, for example, Brower 2014.)

A *quantitative part* of a substance is a part in a very ordinary familiar way, as a finger or a particular pint of blood are parts of an individual organism. Non-quantitative parts of a substance would include the substantial form and the prime matter of the substance, and perhaps also the essence itself (composed of the substantial form and prime matter considered abstractly). I will assume that there is such a thing as prime matter, which is to be understood as a gunky[28] form of bare particularity (Brower 2014, 134). Prime matter in my view plays the role of individuating substances of the same species (which is a controversial stance, even among Aristotelians). However, I don't think anything substantive in this paper depends on this assumption.

28 'Gunk' is a term (introduced by David Lewis) for material things that are infinitely divisible and that contain no indivisible (atomic) parts.

As I mentioned, no substance can have other substances as quantitative parts. To do so would fatally compromise the *per se* unity of the containing substance. The requirements of *per se* unity of the composite substance are so great that we have to think of the quantitative parts as metaphysically dependent on the whole, and not vice versa. The existence and persistence of the parts depends asymmetrically on the existence and persistence of the whole, and the proper accidents of the parts (including their proper causal powers) depend on the essence of the whole (Koons 2014). As a result, Aristotelians seem committed to what has been called The Homonymy Principle: no quantitative part of a substance can exist except as a part of that substance. So, a severed hand is not strictly speaking a hand at all, but only "homonymously" so, the way a picture of a dog is a "dog." Aristotle (1952), *Metaphysics* Zeta (1035b24–5): "For they (the parts of the body) cannot be independently of the whole (animal); since it is not any sort of a finger that is a finger of an animal, a dead finger being a finger in name only." Consequently, no hand of a living organism can survive severance from the body, since each finger is essentially (or quasi-essentially) a finger, while the severed "finger" or the "finger" of a corpse is not. The essence of things, including quantitative parts, is tied to their telic functioning: "When seeing is removed the eye is no longer an eye, except in name." (Aristotle 2017, *De Anima* II.1, 412b10) Once the whole organism is dead, its quantitative parts lose their function. Thomas Aquinas (1954–57) agrees: "Both the whole and the parts take their species from [the substantial form], so when it leaves, neither the whole nor the part remain the same in species. For a dead person's eye and flesh are so called only equivocally." (SCG II.72.1484, Aquinas 1954–57)

7.2 The Persistence of Accidents

Can accidents persist beyond the demise of their substances? There are two cases to consider: accidents of the whole substance, and accidents of quantitative parts of the substance. If quantitative parts of a substance could persist beyond the demise of the whole substance, then the accidents of those parts would also have to exist after the substance's demise. An accident of a quantitative part is in a sense an accident of the whole substance, and so in this way accidents of a substance could persist beyond the substance's demise, if the quantitative part could. I will take up this question in the next session.

Let's turn first to the case of accidents of the whole substance. It *seems* obvious that such an accident could not survive if the substance does not, since an accident is simply the substance's being-a-certain-way (quantitatively, qualitatively, or relatively). As Thomas Aquinas (1995) puts it, "Accidents have a mode of existence such that they cannot exist *per se* but only being-in (something)." (*Commentary on the Metaphysics* VII, L1 par. 1254) If the substance is not actually at all, it cannot actually be a certain way. Aristotle states clearly that color must be in an individual body (*Categories* 2b2). Aquinas writes, "Accidents have no being unless they exist in a subject." (*Commentary on the Metaphysics* VII, L4 par. 1352, Aquinas 1995) They are incapable of independent existence (par. 1291). An accident without its substance would be something very like the smile of the Cheshire cat without the cat.

However, this inference moves too quickly. Do we know that an accident cannot have being "in a subject" when that subject no longer exists (in actuality)? And what does it mean for accidents to lack "independent" existence? Couldn't that mean that it is impossible for an accident to come into existence without receiving that existence from a substance? As Aquinas (1995) wrote (*Commentary on the Metaphysics* VII, L8, 1459, Aquinas 1995), substance is the "active principle" of accidents. It is impossible for accidents to be prior to substances "in definition (ratio), time, or generation." (Op cit. L13, 1579) Accidents do not have "perfect being (*esse perfectum*)" unless they exist in a subject. (L9, 1477) This non-priority of accidents seems compatible with some accidents continuing to exist after their substances have been destroyed.

In addition, John Wippel (Wippel 2000, 253–65) and Stephen Brock (Brock 2014) have argued that every accident has its own act of being (*actus essendi*), an act of accidental being or being-in, which is distinct from but dependent on the act of existence of the whole substance. This at least raises the conceptual possibility of an accident's existing in the absence of the existence of its substance.

In one case, as is well known, Aquinas explicitly affirmed the possibility of the persistence of accidents in the absence of their subjects: the accidents of the Host in the Eucharist (transubstantiation). Aquinas (1947a) discusses this in the *Summa Theologica*, Part III, q77 a1. Aquinas asserts in the second Reply that we cannot simply identify the definition of *accident* with *being in a subject*, although it is a consequence of the definition of accident that they naturally have their existence in a subject. Consequently, it is not a contradiction in terms to say, "This accident is not in a subject."

Nonetheless, Aquinas affirms in the same article that in the common order of nature (*sans* miracle) an accident must be in a subject. So, if we set aside direct exercises of divine power, it is impossible for accidents to persist after their substances have ceased to exist. It seems that this conclusion is grounded in conjectures about the common course of nature that are revisable in the light of new information, without sacrificing anything indispensable to the Aristotelian framework. In other word, the synchronic dependence of accidents on their substances is a secondary rather than primary feature of Aristotelianism.

In addition, there is at least one case of an accident for which this synchronic dependence was not even a secondary postulate: the accidents in the category of *action*. The accident of action exists *in* the patient, even though it is an accident *of* both the agent (and, *qua passion*, the same change is also an accident *of* the patient). In *Physics* 3.3, Aristotle teaches that the action and the passion are the same movement, and that the movement of the patient is the fulfillment or actuality (*entelechia*) of both the agent and patient. This real identity of action and passion, and the identification of both with movement or change in the patient is affirmed also by Aquinas in many places, including *In Physica* III, par. 1268–69, ST I, q 29 a3 ad 1, and ST I, q 45 a2 ad 2 (Aquinas 1958–62).

The action of the agent is not complete until the change in the patient has reached its natural culmination, even if the agent and patient are not in continuous contact, as Aquinas explains in *De Potentia* 3.11 ad 5 (Aquinas 1952):

> An instrument is understood to be moved by a principal agent so long as it retains the power (*virtus*) impressed by the principal agent; whence the arrow is moved by the archer so long the force imparted by the archer remains.... It is necessary that the mover and moved be together at the beginning of the motion, but not for the whole motion, as is evident in projectiles.

Suppose the archer dies before the arrow's motion is complete. In that case, the archer's accident of action persists beyond the duration of the substance's existence. A similar point is acknowledged by Aristotle (2009) in Book I of the *Nicomachean Ethics*. Happiness is a certain kind of activity of a human being. Aristotle writes in Book III of the *Nicomachean Ethics*

(1112b), "Things we do through the agency of our friends counting in a sense as done by ourselves, since the origin of their action is in us." Consequently, events that affect the culmination of someone's actions after that person's death (by affecting activities shared with friends) can affect the dead person's happiness.

Could we suppose in these cases that it is not the original action that produces the later changes (after the demise of the original agent), but rather new actions of new agents—i.e., a chain of distinct agents initiated by the original agent? (Thanks to an anonymous referee for this suggestion.) Three points in response. First, in many cases there is no substitute agent to take over the agential function. The air around the arrow does not make it move as it does. And we know now that an arrow can be shot in a vacuum. Second, since action does not exist in the agent, there is no reason *a priori* to rule out its persistence. And, finally, the action of other agents (like friends) can simultaneously be actions of the original agent.

This is relevant to accommodating modern quantum theory, as I have argued (Koons

2018a, 2019). Quantum particles (photons, electrons, baryons, etc.) are not individual things—they are neither substances nor quantitative parts of substances. Particles are merely aspects of potential actions of the substance that emits them. Substances are not in any sense composed of particles. The picture of atoms as little solar systems inside my body is untenable in light of the quantum revolution. My body is in fact a continuum of matter with the potential to act in quantized ways, and this quantization of action is what makes the metaphor of "particle" occasionally apt.

We see distant stars by virtue of the photons they emitted (that is, by virtue of their quantized photonic actions). Many of the stars we see no longer exist, since it took millions of years for their light to reach us. When we see an extinct star, we are directly acted upon by a substance that no longer exists. The substance no longer exists, but many of its accidents of action (or potential action) do.

What is the defining relationship between substances and their accidents, if accidents can exist after the substance's demise? The relationship is one that requires only that both relata exist in potentiality. It is not necessary for both to exist in actuality. For an accident to exist in actuality, it is necessary for its substance to be actual or *to have been actual in the past*. This is because an accident can receive actual existence only through its substance. A substance can exist in actuality even though there are many potential accidents of that substance that are not, have not been, and will in fact never be actual. So, in the order of actual existence there is an asymmetric dependence of each accident on its substance. But this dependence does not rule out an accident's persisting beyond the demise of its substance.

Accidents have a dual dependence on their substances. As we have seen, every accident must receive its existence at some point in time from a substance. Secondly, each accident is individuated by its substance. Any two accidents of the same type are not fundamentally or primitive distinct from each other. Instead, they derive their mutual numerical distinctness from the numerical distinctness of their substances (Brower 2016, Koons

2018d). This means that the individual identity of each accident is essentially tied to that
of a particular substance. Consequently, no
accident can be transferred from one substance to another. However, that does not rule
out the possibility of an accident existing on
its own, in the absence of its original substance. This is analogous to what Aquinas has
to say about the individuation of human souls
after death: two souls are individuated by
virtue of their relation to two distinct bodies,
even though those bodies no longer exist in
actuality. The past existence of the bodies suffices (SCG II 81, par. 8). Souls are not accidents, but both souls and accidents are
individuated by something else.

How could an accident be actual at a time
if its substance is not? The category of *action*
seems to be the only case in which this could
occur, in the absence of a miracle (except for
the case of accidents of quantitative parts,
which I take up in the following section). This
is because the accident of action exists in a
second substance, the patient. So long as the
patient substance exists, the agent's accident
of passion can exist, even if the agent no

longer does. Therefore, the Aristotelian en-
counters no difficulty in accounting for the
physical actions of substances (in the guise of
emitted particles/waves) that persist after the
demise of the substance.

7.3 The Persistence of Quantitative Parts

Do material substances (like organisms) have
quantitative parts—parts that correspond to
different regions of the space occupied by the
whole substance? This question leads to a potential dilemma. On the one hand, it is the very
nature of quantity to be divisible. In addition,
heterogeneous substances like organisms seem
to be actually divided into disjoint parts,
namely, the body's organs and discrete tissues.
On the other hand, if a substance can be partitioned into a plurality of quantitative parts,
what prevents the substance from being simply
the heap of those parts? What is the relationship between the whole substance and the parts
(taken collectively)? A weird sort of duplication
seems to occur. Both the substance and the parts

taken collectively occupy the same space at the same time. Can the whole do anything over and above what is done by the parts collectively? If not, doesn't the whole become causally redundant (as argued in Merrick 2001)?

Every quantitative accident of a substance should be associated with some portion of prime matter, acting as a "bare particular," a primitive source of individual difference. This should be true of potential parts of the substance's location as well as actual parts. Let's assume that the occupied parts of space include no simples (that is, no points). Then we will have a *gunky* (to use David Lewis's term) continuum of bare particulars associated with each material substance. This gunky continuum could fittingly be called *prime matter*.

Each gob of prime matter is material and underlies some quantitative accident of spatiality. Since these accidents are proper parts of the spatial accidents of the whole substance, there is a material and quantitative *entity* (a particular thing) that is a proper part of the substance. So, material substances have quantitative or material parts. This means that we have to deal with the second horn of the dilemma and answer these questions:

1. How does a material substance differ from a mere heap?
2. When a substance is partitioned into some parts (mutually disjoint and jointly exhaustive of the whole), how is the substance different from the plurality of these parts, taken collectively?
3. If it is different from such a plurality, how can the substance occupy the same space as the parts?
4. What prevents the whole substance from being causally redundant, given the causal powers and potentialities of its parts?

I have dealt with these issues in detail elsewhere (Koons 2014). I will summarize my conclusions here.

1. A material substance differs from a heap by virtue of having a substantial form. The actual existence and the proper accidents (including the causal powers) of all of the quantitative parts of a substance

are grounded by the nature of the one substantial form. The parts receive their actual existence and their nature from the whole.

2. Taking the parts making up a plurality collectively would leave out the one substantial form of the whole.

3. A heterogenous substance (like an organism) occupies space *by virtue of* its actual parts' collectively occupying that space, so there is no objectionable duplication of located things. The parts are enabled to occupy space by virtue of the substantial form of the whole. A homogeneous substance or homogeneous part typically has no actual parts, but only potential ones.

4. The whole substance is the ground for the fundamental causal powers of the parts, so the whole is causally relevant. In addition, in living organisms the substantial form of the whole is the ground for the persistence of certain holistic processes in which multiple parts participate, and these processes alter and coordinate the causal powers of the parts.

Answer 3 places the issue of actual and potential parts on the table. It is essential to Aristotelianism that every substance have only finitely many *actual* parts. Since all of space is divisible without limit, every material body has an infinite number of potential parts. Potential parts (by definition) have only potential existence. Nevertheless, merely potential things are a crucial part of an Aristotelian ontology. They belong to our domain of quantification, so we can truly say, *some things do not actually exist* (namely, those things that are merely potential in being).

Living organisms have a finite number of actual parts, corresponding to the distinct organs and tissues that make up the living body. These parts participate in various holistic processes, such as respiration, immune response, whole-body growth and development, sensory perception, inference, and coordinated bodily movements. The substantial form of the whole organism is the ground for the possible existence and diachronic persistence of these holistic processes, and the processes correspond to a kind of top-down influence on the actions and passions of the parts.

There is a threefold dependence of quantitative parts on whole substances. First, each actual quantitative part receives (at the time of its generation) both its actual existence and its proper nature from the whole. Second, the essence or quasi-essence of each part is defined in terms of its teleological function within the whole. The first dependence ensures that no quantitative part can be initially a part of two distinct substances (since it cannot receive its whole existence at that time from two distinct causes). The second dependence suffices to ensure that the very same quantitative part cannot be successively parts of two different substances. Therefore, each quantitative part is essentially and perpetually the part of a single substance (see Pasnau 2011, 578–87; Cohen 1996, 128–29; Marmodoro 2013). Aquinas (SCG IV, 84, par. 7) states that it is the diachronic numerical identity of the soul (substantial form) that grounds the diachronic identity of the flesh and blood (quantitative parts), and in *Compendium Theologiae*, chapter 153 (Aquinas 1947b), he states that the numerical identity of any proximate matter depends on the numerical identity of the substantial form.

Neither of these two dependencies rules out the part's surviving the demise of the substance. It cannot become part of another substance, but it can continue to exist as a remnant of its original whole.

The third dependence is this: the quantitative accidents of the quantitative parts are accidents of the whole. So, the thesis that quantitative accidents can survive the whole's demise depends on the possibility of accidents doing so, a thesis I defended in the preceding section.

It is possible to keep cells and even whole organs alive, after the organism as a whole has died. If the organism has died, it is impossible to generate a new organ of that same organism, although it is possible to generate new cells, given that the body uses existing cells to generate new ones. Such a process of cell generation can continue after death, as has in fact happened in the case of Henrietta Lacks, whose cells have given rise to cell lines used in laboratories 70 years after her death.

Aristotle (1952) considers such a possibility in Book Zeta of the *Metaphysics* (1040b5–15, reflecting on the fact that some parts of some animals (like worms) seem to be alive (e.g., capable of self-motion) after the animal has been dissected:

> "It is evident that most of the beings that are supposed to be primary are powers (potentialities, *dynameis*). Such are the organs of animals; none of them can be ... separately from its organism, and if separated they continue to be, but as matter.... One might be inclined to suppose that some parts of living bodies and of their living selves (souls, psyche) possess individual being, both actually and potentially, seeing that these parts have a source of movement in them, so that they can move from their normal places, especially in those cases in which animals, even when divided, continue to live. Nevertheless, such parts are only potentially individual beings so long as they are naturally united and continuous...." (Aristotle 1952, 164–65)

Aristotle seems to conclude that such detached organs exist only *potentially*. What could he mean by that? I think he's pointing to the fact that they cannot be substances in their own right. They remain essentially parts (of a certain type) of a particular living organism (matter or *hule* of a certain kind), and they could have perfect existence (to use Aquinas's phrase) only if (*per impossibile*) the living organism of which they are a part were resurrected. Hence, their existence is not *fully* actual. If this is right, then Aristotle is clearly rejecting what Jonathan Schaffer has recently proposed as an Aristotelian postulate: the Tiling Constraint (Schaffer 2010, 38). According to Schaffer's Tiling Constraint, no two substances can have any part in common, and the sum of all substances exhausts the whole of natural or material reality. It is the second part of that constraint that Aristotle seems to reject: there can exist things that are merely remnants of substances, things that are neither substances themselves nor composed of things that are parts of actual substances.

What should we say about organ or tissue transplants? In some cases, we should say that the tissue or organ continues to be a remnant of the original organism, although engineered to mimic a natural function within the recipient. This would happen in the case of relative static or short-lived transplants, like that of blood, bone, or corneas. In other cases, at least potentially, we could say that the original organ has been corrupted and a new (numerically distinct) organ generated in its place by a novel process of digestion or assimilation. As the transplant organ is nourished and even repaired by the recipient's body, a substantial change can occur, in which prime matter is acquired by the recipient's body through continuous processes of locomotion and chemical change that unite the old organ's conditions to that of the new one. This is especially clear when the organ replaces old cells under conditions provided and regulated by the recipient organism.

If quantitative parts of substances can exist as remnants after the substance has corrupted, then such parts can also exist as radicals or mavericks while the whole substance still exists. A paradigm case of this would be cancer cells, which are still clearly parts of the organism's body but no longer fully regulated by the organism's substantial form. Such parts have seceded (at least in part) from the holistic processes that make up the organism's life. They retain their original functions but they no longer fulfill them (at least, not all of them). Such maverick parts play a crucial role in explaining the death of an organism, when there is no external agent. Organisms are not equipped with the active causal power of destroying themselves, since such self-destruction would require the organism to act both as agent and patient. An organism would have to be alive to be the agent of death, and it would have to be dead at the same moment in order to be the patient.

However, nothing prevents a maverick part of an organism from being the agent of the whole organism's death. Cancer cells, for example, can kill their host without directly killing themselves. They can remain as remnants post-death, which is in fact what happened in the case of Henrietta Lacks (the cells in laboratory cultures are actually descendants of some of her cancer cells).

The role of mavericks is also crucial to solving the medieval puzzle that led many late medieval and early modern philosophers to abandon Thomistic Aristotelianism: the brown cow/brown carcass problem (Pasnau 2011, pp. 581–3). When a brown cow dies, its carcass is typically also brown (at least, in the immediate aftermath of death). According to Thomistic Aristotelianism, nothing persists as numerically the same thing through death (except perhaps featureless prime matter). How, then, can the Thomist explain the qualitative and quantitative continuities that we observe?

The correct answer has to involve an appeal to active and passive causal powers. When a butcher kills a cow (say, by decapitating it), the butcher exercises a causal power to produce a carcass that is qualitatively and quantitatively continuous with the living cow, and the living cow has a complementary passive power to be killed and to produce an appropriately quantified and qualified carcass. The only real mystery comes when a cow dies spontaneously, without any external agent. The Thomist cannot appeal to some extrinsically grounded "law of nature" in this case, since it is substantial and accidental forms of substances that are supposed to ground all dynamic laws.

However, the existence of maverick parts resolves the problem. When a cow dies without external agency, it is killed by some of its maverick parts. The active powers of those parts and the passive powers of the cow conspire to produce an appropriately quantified and qualified corpse. No numerical identity of quantitative parts or of accidents is needed.

Parts as persisting remnants thus both solve a number of modern problems generated by contemporary biological knowledge and medical technology and resolve an ancient puzzle that had led many scholastic philosophers to abandon pure Aristotelianism.

7.4 Origin and Individuation of Thermal Substances

How many thermal substances are there? How are they individuated?

For instance, is the earth a single substance? The lithosphere of the earth? The mantle, core, or crust? Tectonic plates? Mountain ranges? Rocks or pebbles? Homogenous crystals? Or are all of these mere *groups* or *heaps* of substances? How many substances does the world's oceans contain? Or the earth's atmosphere? How many substances occupy interplanetary or interstellar space?

In my view, these are open, empirical questions. We cannot settle them from the armchair, or by careful phenomenological examination of ordinary experience. We need to develop full theories of collective phenomena. The study of such phenomena (which physicists term "emergence") is still in its infancy. It is only in the last forty years or so that sustained investigation into these matters has been undertaken. Hylomorphism can be helpful, by ruling out facile, microphysicalist answers, answers that suggest that there is nothing fundamental or deep to study here, since everything is supposedly reducible "in principle" to micro-physics. Ernest Rutherford is reported to have said that all of science is either "atomic physics or stamp collecting." Such microphysical imperialism relegates all the "special" sciences to second-class status, simply arranging on the page facts that are fully explained only by so-called "fundamental" physics.

If hylomorphism true, each of the so-called special sciences is equally fundamental. The world cannot be captured in micro-physical terms alone. The natures and accidents of thermal substances and organisms do not even *supervene on* the character and arrangement of micro-particles. As we descend to the quantum scale, things become *less* definite and *more* dependent, and not the reverse. It is actually quantum physics that is *non*-fundamental, since there are no "quantum substances" per se, but only quantal aspects (accidents) of thermal substances and organisms.

How big can thermal substances be?

Thermal substances can in principle exist at any scale, from single particles (or even fraction of a particle) to the entire cosmos. I conjecture that very small substances are quite short-lived—substances in the late stages of corruption or the early stages of generation.

Very small substances (6 molecules or so) can perhaps be sustained in laboratory conditions. In the wild, they will, I think, generally be much larger.

In the absence of empirical inquiry, I can't answer in detail the questions about the individuation of thermal substances with any confidence, but I can suggest some criteria for individuation:

1. Sharp boundaries or discontinuities, in both space and time (i.e., sharp transitions) are a necessary condition for distinguishing two thermal substances from each other. But such boundaries may not be a sufficient condition. Some thermal substances (like perhaps convection cells) might include some *internal* boundaries. Nonetheless, where there are no sharp boundaries, where there is perfect continuity in temperature, chemical composition, and density, we should count the continuum as contained by a single, enduring substance.

2. Strongly *collective powers* are a *necessary* condition for unity. A substance must have causal powers, both active and passive, that are not determined by the powers and arrangements of its parts. As we have seen, this condition is met by all

bodies with chemical and thermodynamic properties. Again, such strongly collective powers may not be a *sufficient* condition for substantial unity: it could be that a group of substances possesses some strongly collective powers, over and above the powers of the individual substances within it. This happens in the case of human societies, for example.

3. The complete integration of the fundamental or essential causal powers of the parts into the whole is a sufficient condition for unity (at a moment in time). We can make a three-way distinction between substances, heaps, and "groups" of substances. In Thomas's terms, heaps have only the unity of *contiguity*, groups have the unity of *order*, and only substances have *per se* unity. Partial integration of fundamental powers results in *groups*, not in the *per se* unity of a *substance*. In contrast, the parts of a single *substance* are so completely integrated into the nature of the whole that they cannot simultaneously belong in the same way to two distinct wholes. Thus, no two substances can overlap.

Here is an area in which hylomorphism can help scientific investigation into "emergent" phenomena: by focusing research on new and overlooked questions.

Bibliography

Adams, Robert M. (1987), "Flavors, Colors, and God," in *The Virtue of Faith and Other Essays in Philosophical Theology* (New York: Oxford University Press), pp. 243–62.

Aicardi, F., A. Barsellino, G. C. Ghirardi, and R. Grassi (1991), "Dynamical Models for State-Vector Reduction: Do They Ensure that Measurements Have Outcomes?" *Foundations of Physics Letters* 4(2):108–128.

Albert, David Z. (2015), *After Physics* (Cambridge, Mass.: Harvard University Press).

Albert, David Z. and Lev Vaidman (1989), "On a Proposed Postulate of State Reduction," *Physics Letters A* 139(1):1–4.

Amann, Anton (1993), "The Gestalt Problem in Quantum Theory: Generation of

Molecular Shape by the Environment," *Synthese* 97:125–156.

Aquinas, Thomas (1947a), *Summa Theologica*, English Dominican Fathers, trans. (Benziger Brothers).

Aquinas, Thomas (1947b), *Compendium Theologiae*, Cyril Vollert, trans. (St. Louis, MO: B. Herder).

Aquinas, Thomas (1952), *De Potentia*, English Dominican Fathers, trans. (Westminster, MD: Newman Press).

Aquinas, Thomas (1954–57), *Summa Contra Gentiles*, Joseph Kenny, ed. (New York: Hanover House).

Aquinas, Thomas (1958–62), *In Physica*, Pierre Conway, trans. (Columbus OH: College of Mary of the Springs).

Aquinas, Thomas (1995), *Commentary on Aristotle's Metaphysics*, trans. John P. Rowan (Notre Dame, IN: Dumb Ox Books).

Aristotle (1952), *Aristotle's Metaphysics*, Richard Hope, trans. (Ann Arbor: University of Michigan Press).

Aristotle (2009), *Nicomachean Ethics*, David Ross and Lesley Brown, trans. (Oxford: Oxford University Press).

Aristotle (2017), *De Anima*, C. D. C. Reeve, trans. (Indianapolis: Hackett).

Aristotle (1937), *Parts of Animals, Movement of Animals, Progression of Animals*, A. L. Peck and E. S. Forster, trans. (Cambridge, MA: Loeb Classical Library).

Armstrong, David M. (1996), *A World of States of Affairs* (Cambridge, UK: Cambridge University Press).

Armstrong, David M. (1999), *The Mind-Body Problem* (Boulder, CO: Westview Press).

Bacon, Francis (1915), *The Advancement of Learning* (London: Dent).

Bangu, Sorin (2009), "Understanding thermo-dynamic singularities: phase transitions, data and phenomena," *Philosophy of Science* 76:488–505.

Barrett, Jeffrey A. (1995), "The single-mind and many-minds versions of quantum mechanics," *Erkenntnis* 42:89–105.

Bibliography

Bell, J. S. (1987), *Speakable and Unspeakable in Quantum Mechanics* (Cambridge: Cambridge University Press).

Bernard, Claude (1966), *Lecons sur les phenomenes de la vie commune aux animaux et aux vegetaux* (Paris: Libraire Philosophique J. Vrin).

Bishop, Robert C. and Harald Atmanspacher (2006), "Contextual Emergence in the Description of Properties," *Foundations of Physics* 36:1753–1777.

Bogen, Jim and James Woodward (1988), "Saving the Phenomena," *Philosophical Review* 97:303–352.

Bohm, David (1951), *Quantum Theory*, (Englewood Cliffs, NJ: Prentice-Hall).

Brentano, Franz (1988), *Philosophical Investigations on Space, Time and the Continuum*, Stephen Körner and Roderick M. Chisholm, eds., Barry Smith, trans., (London: Croom Helm).

Broad, C. D. (1925), *The Mind and Its Place in Nature* (London: Kegan Paul, Trench and Trubner).

Brock, Stephen L. (2014), "How Many Acts of Being Can a Substance Have? An Aristotelian Approach to Aquinas's Real Distinction," *International Philosophical Quarterly* 54(3):317–31.

Brower, Jeffrey E. (2014), *Aquinas's Ontology of the Material World* (Oxford: Oxford University Press).

Brower, Jeffrey E. (2016), "Aquinas on the Problem of Universals," *Philosophy and Phenomenological Research* 92(3): 715–35, DOI: 10.1111/phpr.12176.

Brower, Jeffery E. (2017), "Aquinas on the Individuation of Substances," *Oxford Studies in Medieval Philosophy* 5(1) DOI:10.1093/oso/9780198806035.003.0004.

Brown, H. R., C. Dewdney, and G. Horton (1995), "Bohm Particles and Their Detection in the Light of Neutron Interferometry," *Foundations of Physics* 25(2):329–347.

Brown, Harvey R. and David Wallace (2005), "Solving the measurement problem: de

Broglie-Bohm loses out to Everett," *Foundations of Physics* 35:517–540.

Butterfield, Jeremy (2011), "Less is Different: Emergence and Reduction Reconciled," *Foundations of Physics* 41: 1065–1135.

Campbell, Keith (1990), *Abstract Particulars* (Oxford: Basil Blackwell).

Cartwright, Nancy (1994), *Nature's Capacities and their Measurement* (Oxford: Clarendon Press).

Cartwright, Nancy (1999), *The Dappled World: A Study of the Boundaries of Science* (Cambridge: Cambridge University Press).

Clifton, Robert and Hans Halvorson (2001), "Entanglement and open systems in algebraic quantum field theory," *Studies in History and Philosophy of Modern Physics* 32:1–31.

Cohen, Sheldon M. (1996), *Aristotle on Nature and Incomplete Substances* (Cambridge: Cambridge University Press).

Compagner, Aaldert (1989), "Thermodynamics as the continuum limit of statistical mechanics," *American Journal of Physics* 57 (2):106–117.

Cross, Richard (1998), *The Physics of Duns Scotus: The Scientific Context of a Theological Vision* (Oxford: Clarendon Press).

Dancy, Jonathan (2003), *Practical Reality* (Oxford: Oxford University Press).

Davidson, Donald (1973), "Radical interpretation," *Dialectica*, 27:314–28, 1973.

Dawkins, Richard (1976), *The Selfish Gene* (Oxford: Oxford University Press).

De Koninck, Charles (1934), *Le Cosmos* (Québec: Imprimerie Franciscaine Missionnaire).

Dennett, Daniel C. (1991), "Real Patterns," *Journal of Philosophy* 88(1):27–51.

Descartes, Rene (1973), *Discourse on the Method of Rightly Conducting the Reason*, trans. Elizabeth Haldane and G. R. T. Ross, *The Philosophical Works of Descartes*, Volume I (Cambridge: Cambridge University Press).

Deutsch, David (1999), "Quantum theory of probability and decisions," *Proceedings of the Royal Society of London* A455:3129–37.

Dewdney, C., L. Hardy, and E. J. Squires (1993), "How late measurements of quantum trajectories can fool a detector," *Phys. Lett.* 184A, 6–11.

DeWitt, B. and N. Graham (1973), *The Many-Worlds Interpretation of Quantum Mechanics*, (Princeton, NJ: Princeton University Press).

Drossel, Barbara (2015), "On the relation between the second law of thermodynamics and classical and quantum mechanics," in *Why More Is Different: Philosophical Issues in Condensed Matter Physics and Complex Systems*, B. Falkenburg and M. Morrison, eds. Berlin: Springer, pp 41–54.

Drossel, Barbara and George Ellis (2018), "Contextual Wavefunction Collapse: An integrated theory of quantum measurement," *New Journal of Physics* 20:113025. doi.org/10.1088/1367-2630/aaeccec.

Dürr, Detlef, W. Fussender, Sheldon Goldstein, and Nino Zanghi (1993),

"Comment on 'Surrealistic Bohm Trajectories'," *Zietschrift für Naturforschung* 48a:1261–1262.

Dusek, Val (2001), "Aristotle's Four Causes and Contemporary 'Newtonian' Dynamics," in *Aristotle and Contemporary Science*, vol. 2, D. Sfendoni-Mentzou, J. Harriangadi and D. M. Johnson (eds.), Peter Lang, New York, pp. 81–93.

Earman, John (2004), "Curie's Principle and Spontaneous Symmetry Breaking," *International Studies in Philosophy of Science* 18:173–198.

Emch, Gérard G. and Chuang Liu (2005), "Explaining spontaneous symmetry breaking," *Studies in History and Philosophy of Modern Physics* 36(1):137–163.

Englert, B.-G., M. O. Scully, G. Süssman, and H. Walther (1992), "Surrealistic Bohm trajectories," *Zeitschrift für Naturforschung* 47a, 1175–1186.

Esfeld, Michael (2017), "A Proposal for a Minimalist Ontology," *Synthese* https://doi-org.ezproxy.lib.utexas.edu/10.1007/s11229-017-1426-8.

Bibliography

Everett, Hugh III (1957). "'Relative state' formulation of quantum mechanics," *Reviews of Modern Physics* 82:1575–1646.

Feyerabend, Paul (1983), "Foreword," in Primas (1983), pp. i-xii.

Fine, Kit (1999), "Things and Their Parts," *Midwest Studies in Philosophy* 23: 61–74.

Fine, Kit (2012). "Guide to Ground," in Fabrice Correia and Benjamin Schnieder, eds., *Metaphysical Grounding: Understanding the Structure of Reality* (Cambridge: Cambridge University Press), pp. 37–80.

Fraser, Doreen (2008), "The Fate of 'Particles' in Quantum Field Theories with Interactions," *Studies in History and Philosophy of Modern Physics* 39:841–59.

Gell-Mann, M. and J. B. Hartle (1990), *Quantum mechanics in the light of quantum cosmology. In Complexity, Entropy, and the Physics of Information* (Boston: Addison-Wesley).

Gell-Mann, M. and J. B. Hartle (1993), "Classical equations for quantum systems," *Physical Review* D47:3345–82.

Ghirardi, G.C., Rimini, A., and Weber, T. (1985), "A Model for a Unified Quantum Description of Macroscopic and Microscopic Systems," *Quantum Probability and Applications*, L. Accardi et al., eds. (Berlin: Springer.)

Gibson, J. J. (1979), *The Ecological Approach to Visual Perception* (Boston: Houghton-Mifflin).

Gilson, Etienne (1984), *From Aristotle to Darwin and Back Again: A Journey in Final Causation, Species, and Evolution*, John Lyon, trans. (Notre Dame, IN: University of Notre Dame Press).

Griffiths, R. (1984), "Consistent histories and the interpretation of quantum mechanics," *Journal of Statistical Physics* 36:219–72, 1984.

Grove, Stanley F. (2008), *Quantum Theory and Aquinas's Doctrine on Matter*, Ph.D. dissertation, Catholic University of America.

Healey, Richard (1991), "Holism and nonseparability," *Journal of Philosophy* 88(8):393–421.

Heisenberg, Werner (1958), *Physics and Philosophy: The Revolution in Modern Science* (London: George Allen and Unwin).

Hendry, Robin Findlay (2006), "Is There Downward Causation in Chemistry?" In *Philosophy of Chemistry: Synthesis of a New Discipline*, D. Baird, E. Scerri, and L. McIntyre, eds. (Dordrecht: Springer), pp. 173–189.

Hiley, B. J., R. E. Callaghan, and O. J. Maroney (2000), "Quantum trajectories, real, surreal or an approximation to a deeper process?" quant-ph/00100220 v2.

Humphreys, Paul (1997), "How properties emerge," *Philosophy of Science* 64:1–17.

Inman, Ross D. (2018), *Substance and the Familiarity of the Familiar: A Neo-Aristotelian Mereology* (New York: Routledge).

Kadanoff, Leo P. (2009), "More is the same: phase transitions and mean field theories," *Journal of Statistical Physics* 137:777–797.

Kadanoff, Leo P. (2013), "Theories of Matter: Infinities and Renormalization,"

Oxford Handbook of Philosophy of Physics, Robert Batterman, ed. (Oxford: Oxford University Press), pp. 141–188.

Koons, Robert C. (2014), "Staunch vs. Fainthearted Hylomorphism: Toward an Aristotelian Account of Composition," *Res Philosophica* 91:1–27.

Koons, Robert C. (2017), "The Epistemological and Ontological Superiority of Hylomorphism," *Synthese* doi:10.1007/s11229-016–1295–6.

Koons, Robert C. (2018a), "Hylomorphic Escalation: A Hylomorphic Interpretation of Quantum Thermodynamics and Chemistry," *American Catholic Philosophical Quarterly* 92:159–78.

Koons, Robert C. (2018b), "The Many Worlds Interpretation of Quantum Mechanics: A Hylomorphic Critique and Alternative," in *Neo-Aristotelian Perspectives on Contemporary Science*, William Simpson, Author, and Nicholas Teh, eds. (London: Routledge).

Koons, Robert C. (2018c), "Aristotle, God, and the Quantum," in *Knowing Creation:*

Bibliography

Perspectives from Theology, Philosophy, and Science, Andrew Torrance and Thomas H. McCall, eds. (New York: Harper-Collins).

Koons, Robert C. (2018d), "Forms as Simple and Individual Grounds of Things' Natures," *Metaphysics* 1(1):1–11, DOI: https://doi.org/10.5334/met.4.

Koons, Robert C. (2019a), "Thermal Substances: A Neo-Aristotelian Ontology for the Quantum World," *Synthese*. doi:10.1007/s11229-019-02318-2.

Koons, Robert C. (2019b), "Hylomorphism and our Knowledge of Value," in *Being, Goodness, and Truth: Proceedings of the Society for Medieval Logic and Metaphysics*, volume 16, Alex Hall, ed. (Newcastle upon Tyne: Cambridge Scholars Publishing), pp. 78–90.

Koons, Robert C. (2021), "Powers ontology and the quantum revolution." *European Journal for Philosophy of Science* 11(1):1–28.

Koons, Robert C. and Pruss, Alexander R. (2017). "Must a Functionalist be an

Aristotelian?" in *Causal Powers*, Jonathan D. Jacobs, ed. (Oxford: Oxford University Press), pp. 194–204.

Koons, Robert C. and Pickavance, Timothy H. (2017), *The Atlas of Reality: A Comprehensive Guide to Metaphysics* (Malden, MA: Wiley Blackwell).

Korsgaard, Christina M. (1986), "Scepticism about Practical Reason," *Journal of Philosophy* 83:5–25.

Kronz, Frederick and Justin Tiehen (2002), "Emergence and quantum mechanics." *Philosophy of Science* 69:324–347.

Kronz, Frederick M. and Tracy A. Lupher (2005), "Unitarily Inequivalent Representations in Algebraic Quantum Theory," *International Journal of Theoretical Physics* 44(3):1239–1258.

Lanczos, Cornelius (1986), *The Variational Principles of Mechanics*, 4th edition (New York: Dover Publications).

Lee, Patrick and Robert P. George (2009), *Body-Self Dualism in Contemporary Ethics and Politics* (Cambridge: Cambridge University Press).

Levine, J. (2000), *Purple Haze: The Puzzle of Conscious Experience* (Cambridge, MA: The MIT Press).

Lewis, C. S. (1947), *Miracles: A Preliminary Study* (London: Centenary Press).

Lewis, David K. (1966), "An argument for identity theory," *Journal of Philosophy* 63:17–25.

Lewis, David K. (1972), "Psychophysical and theoretical identifications," *Australasian Journal of Philosophy* 50:249–258.

Lewis, David K. (1973), *Counterfactuals* (Cambridge, Mass.: Harvard University Press).

Lewis, David K. (1980), "Mad pain and Martian pain," in *Readings in the Philosophy of Psychology*, volume I, Ned Block ed. (Cambridge, Mass.: Harvard University Press), pp. 216–22.

Lewis, David K. (1984), "Putnam's paradox," *Australasian Journal of Philosophy* 62:221–36.

Lindsay, Robert Bruce and Henry Morgenaw (1957), *Foundations of Physics* (New York: Dover Publications).

Liu, Chuang (1999), "Explaining the Emergence of Cooperative Phenomena," *Philosophy of Science* 66 (Proceedings):S92–S106.

Loux, Michael (2008), *Primary Ousia: An Essay on Aristotle's Metaphysics Z and H* (Ithaca, NY: Cornell University Press).

Lowe, E. J. (1992), "The problem of psycho-physical causation," *Australasian Journal of Philosophy* 70(3):263–276, DOI: 10.1080/00048409212345161.

Mackie, J. L. (1977), *Ethics: Inventing Right and Wrong* (Harmondsworth: Penguin).

Mainwood, Paul (2006), *Is More Different? Emergent Properties in Physics*, D. Phil., Oxford University.

Malament, David (1996), "In Defense of Dogma: Why There Cannot Be a Relativistic Quantum Mechanical Theory of (Localizable) Particles," In Robert Clifton (ed.), *Perspectives on Quantum Reality*, (Dordrecht: Springer), pp. 1–10.

Marmodoro, Anna (2013), "Aristotle's Hylomorphism without Reconditioning," *Philosophical Inquiry* 36(1–2):5–22.

Maudlin, Tim (2011), *Quantum Non-Locality and Relativity: Metaphysical Intimations of Modern Physics*, 3rd edition (Chichester: Wiley-Blackwell).

McDonough, Jeffrey K. (2008), "Leibniz's Two Realms Revisited," *Nôus* 42: 673–696.

McDonough, Jeffrey K. (2009), "Leibniz on Natural Teleology and the Laws of Optics," *Philosophy and Phenomenological Research* 78: 505–544.

Menon, Tarun and Craig Callender (2013), "Turn and Face the Strange… Ch-ch-changes: Philosophical Questions Raised by Phase Transitions," In *Oxford Handbook of Philosophy of Physics*, Robert Batterman, ed. (Oxford: Oxford University Press), pp. 189–233.

Millikan, Ruth Garrett (1984), *Language Truth and Other Biological Categories* (Cambridge, Mass.: The MIT Press).

Molnar, George (2003), *Powers: A Study in Metaphysics* (Oxford: Clarendon Press).

Newman, H. A. (1928). Mr. Russell's "Causal theory of perception," *Mind* 37:137–48.

O'Connor, Timothy (1994), "Emergent Properties," *American Philosophical Quarterly* 31:91–104.

O'Connor, Timothy and Hong Yu Wong (2005), "The Metaphysics of Emergence," *Nôus* 39:658–78.

Omnès, R. (1988), "Logical reformulation of quantum mechanics," *Journal of Statistical Physics* 53:893–975.

Pasnau, Robert (2011), *Metaphysical Themes: 1274–1671* (Oxford: Clarendon Press).

Pickstock, C. J. C. (2015), "Matter and mattering: the metaphysics of Rowan Williams," *Modern Theology* 31(4):599–617.

Planck, Max (1936), "Science and Faith," In *Scientific Autobiography and Other Papers*, W. H. Johnsonm trans. (New York: W. W. Norton & Co.).

Planck, Max (1960), "The Principle of Least Action," In *A Survey of Physical Theory*, R. Jones and D. H. Williams, trans. (New York: Dover Publications), pp. 69–81.

Plantinga, Alvin (1993), *Warrant and Proper Function* (New York: Oxford University Press).

Plantinga, Alvin (2003), "Probability and Defeaters," *Pacific Philosophical Quarterly* 84:291–98.

Plantinga, Alvin (2011), *Where the Conflict Really Lies Science, Religion, and Naturalism* (Oxford: Oxford University Press).

Plato (2002), *Five Dialogues*, 2nd ed., G. M. A Grube and John M. Cooper, trans. (Indianapolis, IN: Hackett).

Plato (2014), *Theaetetus*, John McDowell, ed. (Oxford: Oxford University Press).

Prigogine, Ilya (1997), *The End of Certainty: Time, Chaos, and the New Laws of Nature* (New York: Free Press).

Primas, Hans (1980), "Foundations of Theoretical Chemistry," In *Quantum Dynamics for Molecules: The New Experimental Challenge to Theorists*, R G. Woolley, ed. (New York: Plenum Press), pp. 39–114.

Primas, Hans (1983), *Chemistry, Quantum Mechanics, and Reductionism: Perspectives in Theoretical Chemistry* (Berlin: Springer-Verlag).

Primas, Hans (1990a), "Mathematical and

Philosophical Questions in the Theory of Open and Macroscopic Quantum Systems," in Arthur I. Miller, ed., *Sixty-Two Years of Uncertainty: Historical, Philosophical, and Physical Inquiries into the Foundations of Quantum Mechanics* (New York: Plenum Press, 1990), pp. 233–258.

Primas, Hans (1990b), "Induced Nonlinear Time Evolution of Open Quantum Objects," in Arthur I. Miller, ed., *Sixty-Two Years of Uncertainty: Historical, Philosophical, and Physical Inquiries into the Foundations of Quantum Mechanics* (New York: Plenum Press, 1990), pp. 259–280.

Pruss, Alexander R. (2015a), Personal communication.

Pruss, Alexander R. (2015b). Everettian quantum mechanics and functionalism about mind. http://alexanderpruss.blogspot.com/2015/05/everettian-quantum-mechanics-and.html

Pruss, Alexander R. (2018), "A Traveling Forms Interpretation of Quantum Mechanics," in

Bibliography

Neo-Aristotelian Perspectives on Contemporary Science, Robert C. Koons, William M. R. Simpson, and Nicholas The, eds. (London: Routledge), pp. 105–22.

Putnam, Hilary (1978), *Meaning and the Moral Sciences* (London: Routledge & Kegan Paul).

Putnam, Hilary (1980), "Models and Reality," *Journal of Symbolic Logic* 45:464–482.

Putnam, Hilary (1981). *Reason, Truth, and History* (Cambridge: Cambridge University Press).

Ramsey, F. P. (1929), "Theories," In R. B. Braithwaite, editor, *The Foundations of Mathematics and other Logical Essays* (Totowa, NJ: Littlefield and Adams), pp. 212–36.

Rosen, Gideon (2010). "Metaphysical dependence: Grounding and reduction," In B Hale and A. Hoffman, editors, *Modality: Metaphysics, Logic, and Epistemology*, pp. 109–36 (Oxford: Oxford University Press).

Rota, Michael (2011), "Causation," in *The*

Oxford Handbook of Aquinas, Brian Davies & Eleonore Stump, eds. (Oxford: Oxford University Press), pp. 104–114.

Ruetsche, Laura (2006), "Johnny's So Long at the Ferromagnet," *Philosophy of Science* 73:473–486.

Ruetsche, Laura (2011), *Interpreting Quantum Theories: The Art of the Possible* (Oxford: Oxford University Press).

Russell, Bertrand (1927), *The Analysis of Matter* (London: K. Paul, Trench, Trubner & Co.).

Sanz, A. S. and F. Borondo (2003), "A Quantum Trajectory Description of Decoherence," quant-ph/0310096.

Scaltas, Theodore (1994), "Substantial Holism," in *Unity, Identity, and Explanation in Aristotle's Metaphysics*, Theodore Scaltsas, David Charles, and Mary Louise Gill (eds.) (Oxford: Clarendon Press), pp. 107–128.

Schaffer, Jonathan (2010), "Monism: The Priority of the Whole," *Philosophical Review* 119: 31–76.

Schlosshauer, Maximilian (2005), "Decoherence, the measurement problem, and the interpretation of quantum mechanics," *Rev Mod. Phys*. 76:1268–1305.

Schulman, Adam L. (1989), "Quantum and Aristotelian Physics," Ph.D. dissertation, Harvard University.

Sellars, Wilfrid (1962), "Philosophy and the scientific image of man," In Robert Colodny, editor, *Frontiers of Science and Philosophy*, pp. 35–78 (Pittsburgh: University of Pittsburgh Press).

Sewell, G. L. (1986), *Quantum Theory of Collective Phenomena* (Oxford: Clarendon Press).

Sewell, Geoffrey L. (2002), *Quantum Mechanics and its Emergent Macrophysics* (Princeton, N. J.: Princeton University Press).

Silberstein, Michael and John McGeever (1999), "The Search for Ontological Emergence," *Philosophical Quarterly* 49:182–200.

Simpson, William M. R. (2018), "Half-baked Humeanism," in *Neo-Aristotelian Perspectives on Contemporary Science,* ed. William M. R. Simpson, Author, and Nicholas Teh, New York: Routledge pp. 123–145.

Simpson, William M. R. (2020), *What's the Matter? Toward a Neo-Aristotelian Ontology of Nature*, unpublished doctoral dissertation, Peterhouse, University of Cambridge.

Simpson, W. M. R. (2021a), "Cosmic hylomorphism: a powerist ontology for quantum mechanics," *European Journal for Philosophy of Science* 11(1):1–25.

Simpson, William M. R. (2021b) "What's the Matter with Super-Humeanism?" *British Journal for the Philosophy of Science* 72(3):893-911, doi 10.1093/bjps/axz028.

Simpson, William M. R. (2022), "From Quantum Physics to Classical Metaphysics," in *Neo-Aristotelian Metaphysics and the Theology of Nature*, Robert C. Koons, William M. R. Simpson, and James Orr, eds. (New York: Routledge), pp. 21–65.

Simpson, William M. R. (forthcoming), *Hylomorphism* (Cambridge: Cambridge University Press).

Smith, Wolfgang (2005), *The Quantum Enigma: Finding the Hidden Key*, 3rd edition (San Rafael, Calif.: Angelico Press).

Steward, Helen (2012), *A Metaphysics for Freedom* (Oxford: Oxford University Press).

Stone, A. D. (1994), "Does the Bohm theory solve the measurement problem?" *Philosophy of Science* 62: 250–266.

Strocchi, Franco (1985), *Elements of Quantum Mechanics of Infinite Systems* (Singapore: World Scientific).

Tahko, Tuomas E. (2018), "Disentangling Nature's Joints," in *Neo-Aristotelian Perspectives on Contemporary Science*, ed. Robert C. Koons William M. R. Simpson, and Nicholas Teh (New York: Routledge), pp. 147–166.

Teller, Paul (1986), "Relational Holism and Quantum Mechanics," *British Journal for the Philosophy of Science* 37 (1):71–81.

Thalos, Mariam (2013), *Without Hierarchy: The Scale Freedom of the Universe* (Oxford: Oxford University Press).

Toepfer, Georg (2012), "Teleology and its constitutive role for biology as the science of organized systems in nature," *Studies in History and Philosophy of Science Part*

C: *Studies in History and Philosophy of Biological and Biomedical Sciences* 43: 113–119.

van Inwagen, Peter (1990). *Material Beings* (Ithaca: Cornell University Press).

Vemulapalli, G. Krishna and Henry Byerly (1999), "Remnants of Reductionism," *Foundations of Chemistry* 1:17–41.

von Neumann, John (1931), "Die Eindeutigkeit der Schrödingerschen Operatoren," *Mathematische Annalen* 104: 570–588.

Wallace, David (2008), "Philosophy of Quantum Mechanics," in *The Ashgate Companion to Contemporary Philosophy of Physics*, ed. Dean Rickles (Oxford: Routledge), pp. 16–98.

Wallace, David (2011), *The Emergent Multiverse* (Oxford: Oxford University Press).

Wippel, John F. (2000), *The Metaphysical Thought of Thomas Aquinas: From Finite Being to Uncreated Being* (Washington, DC: Catholic University of America Press).

Woolley, R. G. (1988), "Quantum Theory and the Molecular Hypothesis," In: *Molecules in Physics, Chemistry, and Biology*, Vol. I, Jean Maruani, ed. (Kluwer Academic: Dordrecht, pp. 45–89.

Yourgrau, Wolfgang and Stanley Mandelstam (1968), *Variational Principles in Dynamics and Quantum Theory*, 3rd ed. (Philadelphia: Saunders).

Zeh, D. (1973), "Toward a quantum theory of observation," *Foundations of Physics* 3:109–16, 1973.

Zurek, W. H. (1982), "Environment-induced superselection roles," *Physical Review* D26:1862–80.